Case Scenarios for Teaching and Learning Social Work Practice

Editors

Shirley M. Haulotte
Jane A. Kretzschmar

Contributing Authors

Eunice C. Garcia
Bonnie L. Bain
Jean E. Avera
Kathy F. Armenta

Council on Social Work Education
Alexandria, Virginia

Teaching Social Work:
Resources for Educators

Library of Congress Cataloging-in-Publication Data

Case scenarios for teaching and learning social work practice / editors, Shirley M. Haulotte, Jane A. Kretzschmar; contributing authors, Eunice C. Garcia . . . [et al.].
    p. cm. -- (Teaching social work)
  Includes bibliographic references.
  ISBN 0-87293-082-3
  1. Social work education. 2. Social case work.   I. Haulotte, Shirley M., 1944-   .   II. Kretzschmar, Jane A., 1956- . III. Garcia, Eunice. IV. Title. V. Series.
  HV11.C33 2001
  361.3'071--dc21   00-013114

Manufactured in the United States of America

Contents

Contents by Topic/Issue

Involuntary

Male

Mental Health

Native American

Organization/Community

Poverty

Public Welfare

Religion/Spirituality

Rural

School

Substance Abuse

Teen Pregnancy/Parenting

Violence/Abuse

Preface

This collection of case vignettes is designed to help social workers examine methods of intervention with clients from diverse populations in a variety of situations. The book is designed for social work educators, students, and field instructors. However, practitioners in many areas of social work would benefit from the vignettes, Suggested Activities, and Recommended Readings. The cases encompass a broad spectrum of agency-based social work. Client systems range from the newborn to the 90-year-old; agencies from the corporation to the two-person office; situations from micro to macro systems.

Through each vignette, the reader is invited to assess the information provided and to begin to formulate an intervention plan. In an attempt to be representative of the helping process, some of the cases portray the first time a client seeks services, others portray situations further along in the helping process, and some show moments close to the termination phase. All the vignettes are drawn from actual cases, although the names and details have been altered for purposes of confidentiality.

This casebook has been written in response to a need expressed by social work educators for a tool that is easily adapted to the classroom or field setting. The cases are intended to augment students' application of classroom material to an assortment of cases, broadening their awareness of client populations and situations. The material in the vignettes is meant to challenge the reader to utilize the perspective of an agency-based social worker rather than that of a social work student in order to begin to look at best practices in the field.

The case method of teaching and learning was chosen to provide greater opportunities for reflection and critical thinking. The social work literature supports this method. Perhaps the earliest and most familiar example is Perlman's (1957) Social Casework, in which she uses a number of case examples to illustrate her model. Pincus and Minihan (1973) also used the case method in their generalist approach to social work practice. More recently, Kowalski, Weaver, and Henson (1990) espoused the case study method as one that creates a classroom condition conducive to active learning. Silverman, Welty, and Lyon (1992) emphasize the value of "student-generated analysis," and LeCroy (1999) sees case study as "an opportunity to vicariously participate in the process of doing social work practice" (p. xv). Rivas and Hull (2000) discuss the importance of case method learning that aids "in the more abstract, conceptual work of summarizing and applying critical thinking skills that will reinforce learners' abilities to transfer new information learned to other practice situations encountered in field practicum, and eventually, in professional social work practice" (p. xii).

According to Mosher (1995) "learning is a cooperative effort between students and teachers and should involve active participation of the cognitive, moral and social competencies of the students" (p. 15). Other authors espouse innovative university teaching including "reflection in action" (Cowan, 1998) and learning through critical reflective practice (Ghaye & Ghaye, 1998; Gould & Taylor, 1996). This book is a vehicle for combining the teaching philosophies of these authors and many educators to enhance reflective critical thinking on the part of students.

References

Cowan, T. (1998). On becoming an innovative university teacher: Reflection in action. Philadelphia, PA: Society for Research into Higher Education.

Ghaye, T., & Ghaye, K. (1998). Teaching and learning through critical reflective practice. London: David Fulton.

Gould, N., & Taylor, I. (1996). Reflective learning for social work: Research, theory, and practice. Brookfield, VT: Ashgate.

Kowalski, T., Weaver, R., & Henson, K. (1990). Case studies and teaching. New York: Longman.

LeCroy, C. W. (1999). Case studies in social work practice (2nd ed.). Pacific Grove, CA: Brooks/Cole.

Mosher, R. (1995). Educational and psychological application of theories of human development: A brief overview. Journal of Education, 177(1), 1-15.

Perlman, H. (1957). Social casework: a problem-solving process. Chicago, IL: University of Chicago Press.

Pincus, A., & Minihan, A. (1973). Social work practice: Model and method. Itasca, IL: F. E. Peacock.

Rivas, R. G., & Hull, G. H., Jr. (Eds.). (2000). Case studies in generalist practice (2nd ed.). Belmont, CA: Wadsworth/Thomson Learning.

Silverman, R., Welty, W., & Lyon, S. (1992). Case studies for teacher problem solving. New York: McGraw-Hill.

Acknowledgments

This casebook came to be as a result of our attempts to keep our teaching fresh and relevant to the field. Teaching practice methods and field seminars allow us to bring client stories into the classroom. At the urging of colleagues and friends, we decided to compile these cases into a book for others to use.

There are many to thank for encouragement and ideas. We would like to thank our colleagues in the School of Social Work field program at the University of Texas at Austin: Barbara Anderson, Sonja Berry, Toni Johnson, Tammy Linseisen, Deena Mersky, Keva Miller, Mary Mulvaney, Vicki Packheiser, Ruth Rubio, Tanya Voss, and Carlene Wooley. We would also like to thank other faculty and staff at the University of Texas at Austin School of Social Work: Janet Boes, Diana DiNitto, Cynthia Franklin, Darlene Grant, Ruth McRoy, and Charlene Urwin. We are grateful to our Dean, Barbara W. White, and Associate Dean, Dorothy Van Soest, for creating an atmosphere where we believed this would be possible. Finally, we'd like to express our gratitude to the many social work students and clients whose lives have crossed our paths over the years, as well as to our friends and our families.

Editors

SHIRLEY M. HAULOTTE, MSSW, LMSW-ACP, is a field specialist in the School of Social Work at the University of Texas at Austin, where she teaches practice methods, field, and courses on issues in aging and cultural diversity. She has received numerous awards for her work in long term care.

JANE A. KRETZSCHMAR, MSW, LMSW-ACP, is the Director of Field Education in the School of Social Work at the University of Texas at Austin. She is active in issues of field education at both the state and national level.

Contributing Authors

EUNICE C. GARCIA, MSSW, LMSW-ACP, is a field specialist in the School of Social Work at the University of Texas at Austin, where she teaches practice methods, field, and courses on Mexican-American families, border issues, and developmental disabilities.

BONNIE L. BAIN, MSSW, LMSW-ACP, is a field specialist in the School of Social Work at the University of Texas at Austin, where she teaches practice methods, field, and courses on feminist practice, clinical supervision, and diversity.

JEAN E. AVERA, MSW, LMSW-ACP, is a field specialist in the School of Social Work at the University of Texas at Austin, where she teaches practice methods, field, and courses on community practice and social change.

KATHY F. ARMENTA, MSW, LMSW-ACP, is a field specialist in the School of Social Work at the University of Texas at Austin, where she teaches practice methods, field, and courses on school social work and community practice and social change.

Other Contributors

MELISSA AERNE, LMSW, is a recent Master's level graduate of the School of Social Work at the University of Texas at Austin. She focused on clinical social work and her case studies represent her experiences working with individuals during her first-year internship.

MARY SIX WOMEN BLOUNT, Ph.D., LCSW, is Chairwoman of the Apalachicola Creek Indians.

Her case studies represent her experiences while working with Native-American issues.

JANE JATINEN, MSW, LMSW-ACP was a field specialist in the School of Social Work at the University of Texas at Austin for many years before retiring to North Carolina. Her case studies represent her experiences while working with Child Protective Services.

Introduction

Organization of the Text

There is agreement among social work theorists that the helping process consists of three major phases. While wording and objectives may differ, the social work skills are the same (Hepworth, Rooney, & Larsen, 1997; Locke, Garrison & Winship, 1998; Sheafor, Horejsi & Horejsi, 1994). The three phases in this casebook are termed:

- The Beginning Phase: What to do After You Say Hello
- The Middle Phase: Energizing the Work
- The Ending Phase: Best Laid Plans

The Beginning Phase encompasses aspects of exploring, assessing, and planning and includes relationship-building skills, listening skills, multidimensional assessment, and contracting (Hepworth et al., 1997). Locke, Garrison, and Winship (1998) use the metaphor of life as a story and liken this first phase of the helping process to "telling and exploring the story" (p. 120). Kirst-Ashman and Hull (1999) emphasize processes of engagement and assessment and detail respective activities. Unit I of this text is comprised of vignettes representative of this first stage of the helping process. Six tasks were chosen to represent the Beginning Phase:

- Building Rapport
- Interpreting Roles within The Agency Context
- Collecting Data
- Defining the Problem
- Initial Assessment/Identifying Strengths
- Contracting and Goal Setting

This list is not meant to be comprehensive, but rather representative of the most common elements of work in the beginning phase of the helping process. These elements appear in many texts, but are phrased differently by different authors. For example, building rapport, is referred to as relationship building by Hepworth et al. (1997), collaboration by Poulin (2000), andengagement by Kirst-Ashman and Hull (1999) and by Sheafor et al. (1994). Similarly, contracting and goal setting are called negotiating goals and formulating a contract (Hepworth et al., 1997), determining goals (Poulin, 2000), formalizing a contract (Kirst-Ashman et al., 1999), and planning and contracting (Sheafor et al., 1994).

In choosing these categories, the authors acknowledge a degree of arbitrariness (e.g., the beginning phase of the helping process actually starts before the first meeting with the client, however, the case vignettes deal primarily with initial face-to-face meetings between client and practitioner). Hopefully, any differences in interpretation can be dealt with during the instructional process in the classroom since the casebook is meant to be representative rather than exhaustive in its content.

The Middle Phase, characterized as "describing a preferred reality," enables the client system to base whatever action is to be taken not only on issues of concern, but also on an idea of how things could be different (Locke et al., 1998). Planning and implementation are the highlighted areas in the Kirst-Ashman and Hull (1999) text, in which the authors employ a generalist perspective that integrates a micro, mezzo, and macro approach to social work practice. Cases in Unit II of this text represent the Middle Stage. Using the same rationale as for the Beginning Phase, five tasks were chosen for the Middle Phase:

- Intervention Planning
- Ongoing Assessment
- Implementation
- Planning for Evaluation
- Overcoming Obstacles to Change

The Final Phase, "evaluating outcomes and making transitions," which involves "the learning that both the social worker and the client system gain from their interaction and the transition that takes place in the client system/social worker relationship" (p. 233). Both Hepworth et al. (1997) and Kirst-Ashman and Hull (1999) include evaluation, termination and follow-up in their characterizations of the final stage of the helping process. Unit III cases represent the ending phase. Two tasks were chosen to represent the Final Phase:

- Integrating Change and Acknowledging Gains
- Anticipating the End /The Final Session

Unit IV, Special Issues: Exceptions to the Rule, is intended to highlight specific circumstances that may require social work intervention at any or all of the stages of the helping process.

The table of contents organizes the vignettes in this casebook according to the stages of the helping process as outlined above; readers interested in particular parts of the helping process should be able to easily locate relevant case vignettes. Directly following the table of contents, Contents by Topic/Issue, categorizes the case vignettes according to specific issues and populations for those readers interested in particular topics or client systems.

Vignette Presentation

All of the vignettes in this volume are intended to provide brief descriptions of problems faced by clients or client systems in a wide variety of practice settings.

The agency is briefly described first in each vignette in order to depict the client system within the parameters of agency mandate and functioning. The educator could use the information in this section to demonstrate the importance of the role of the agency in the helping process.

The client system section of each vignette provides salient information about the client. The information is purposefully concise rather than comprehensive to allow for a variety of problem solving strategies.

Special issues in each vignette accent the particular topics of concern in working with the client system in the situation. These issues are topics that could be used for class discussion.

Key concepts and principles highlight some of the social work precepts which may be the basis for didactic information provided to students.

Suggested activities provides a variety of exercises that can be used in the classroom, small groups, individual instruction, or assignments. Some of the activities are designed to be used by the instructor in the classroom and others are directed to the student or practitioner. Most activities are adaptable to a variety of educational settings.

References and recommended readings contains references to texts cited and recommended reading relevant to the client population represented in the vignette.

Cultural Diversity

Factors of cultural diversity are elements integral to any social work assessment. Although it is preferable to include detailed individual differences in the vignettes, the editors were bound by their attempt to make the cases applicable in all areas of the United States. This resulted in some compromise in the richness of cultural/ethnic/regional differences. Therefore, readers are encouraged to reflect on their particular area of the country and how regional circumstances may influence the client system and practitioner.

In addition, the editors recognize that the terms used by our society for racial demarcation continue to be characterized by indefiniteness, fluidity, and arbitrariness. While one person may prefer the term African-American, others may identify themselves as Black; Anglo is preferred by some and others choose white or some sub-group (e.g., German-American). This complexity is further compounded by the use of terms such as Asian American, Mexican American, Hispanic, and Native American which confer artificial uniformity on disparate groups.

Because questions of racial and ethnic identification are so complex, we urge social workers to remember to *ask* how an individual prefers to be addressed, and listen to the importance that the individual gives to self identity before using any identifying labels.

References

Hepworth, D. H., Rooney, R. H., & Larsen, J. A. (1997). *Direct social work practice: Theory and skills* (5th ed.). Pacific Grove, CA: Brooks/Cole.

Kirst-Ashman, K. K., & Hull, H. H., Jr. (1999). *Understanding generalist practice* (2nd ed.). Chicago, IL: Nelson-Hall.

Locke, B., Garrison, R., & Winship, J. (1998). *Generalist social work practice: Context, story, and partnerships.* Pacific Grove, CA: Brooks/Cole.

Poulin, J. (2000). *Collaborative social work: Strengths-based generalist practice.* Itasca, IL: F. E. Peacock.

Sheafor, B., Horejsi, C. R., & Horejsi, G. A. (1994). *Techniques and guidelines for social work practice* (3rd ed.). Needham Heights, MA: Allyn and Bacon.

Unit I

The Beginning Phase: What to Do After You Say Hello

Chapter 1

Building Rapport

Building rapport is the intentional development of a relationship by the worker, usually based on empathic, active listening to the client's concerns.

Strength Under Fire

The Agency

You are a social worker in a small, private, nonprofit agency serving children with cancer and their families. Clients are in various stages of coping with the impact of having a seriously or terminally ill child. The agency provides a range of services that includes working with the patients and other family members both at the hospital and at home. Support groups, grief and bereavement groups, sibling programs, and "Mom's Night Out" are among the services that are available. It is possible for families to be followed from diagnosis, through several remissions, through death and bereavement.

The Client System

Teresa (age 33) is a white woman from a rural area where she grew up as one of 11 children. Her parents are traditional, second-generation German Americans. Teresa left school in the 7th grade and moved in with her boyfriend's family when she was 16 years old. Teresa maintains that she was a virgin until she and Carl married at 18, but her mother believed that Teresa had disgraced the family. Stephanie was born the first year of Teresa and Carl's marriage, and as soon as Teresa became pregnant for the second time, Carl began seeing other women. Teresa had separated from Carl and moved back home with her parents by the time Emily was born. A third child, Lewis, was the result of one night's sexual encounter. She never saw Lewis' father again.

Teresa entered the welfare system and relied on Temporary Assistance for Needy Families (TANF), Supplemental Security Income (SSI), food stamps, and Medicaid for support. She met a man who has been a loyal friend, supporter, and lover who now lives with Teresa and her children, but does not attempt to co-parent. Teresa maintains frequent, close contact with her extended family, who are now another source of support.

About a year ago Teresa took her middle child, Emily, to the city/county hospital for a persistent cough and cold. Emily was given a preliminary diagnosis of leukemia, later confirmed more specifically as acute myelogenous leukemia. Emily's physician subsequently referred Teresa to a small, non-profit agency, which serves children with cancer and their families.

The family was assigned to you three months after the initial diagnosis, having been transferred from the caseload of another worker. The information available has been gleaned from the previous worker and from one visit with Teresa.

The school and hospital perceive Teresa as passive and lazy, not always reliable in following through with medical protocol or relying on the school to "do everything." From Teresa's perspective, the problems are "others" who try to control her financially and, to some extent, control the health of her child. She is also worried that Stephanie is at risk of dropping out of school at age 14, and that Emily may stop responding to treatment and die. Currently Emily has been in remission for three months.

Special Issues

An obvious issue is how to decide where to intervene first. Systems theory helps in that decision in it's perspective that there are many different, equally effective places to begin in working with clients. A basic social work principle is helpful: Start where the client is.

Another issue is how to be sensitive in working with Teresa and the importance of the role of the social worker in attempting to humanize what is often a very sterile, mainstream medical approach to health care. How can Teresa be empowered to advocate for herself and her child so that Emily will be able to fully benefit from medical science without sacrificing family or traditional values?

When clients are not cooperative it is sometimes a challenge to keep a strengths perspective. With the many stresses and troubles in Teresa's life, it will be important for the worker to recognize and validate her many strengths in coping with them.

Key Concepts and Principles

Involving the client in problem identification

An important social work principle. If a client does not perceive a problem, then motivation for engaging in the client-worker partnership will be minimal.

Natural support systems

In assessing strengths, the client's informal family and community relationships should not be overlooked. Natural support systems may be even more crucial with clients who do not have access to, or do not wish to access, more formal service delivery systems.

Strengths perspective

The concept that symptoms or behavior "problems" may be adaptive (or were once adaptive) helps clients judge themselves less harshly. Workers should also call attention to what is going well, (i.e., the positives in the client and client's situation) rather than focusing only on problems or troubles.

Suggested Activities

1. Role play the initial session with Teresa with the goal of understanding her perspective and clarifying your role in working with her.

2. In small groups, reflect on and discuss the following questions, and then report back to the larger class. What information in this vignette speaks to traditional family values and how can the worker demonstrate respect for them? What is the common denominator in the stated problems and why is that significant? How might Teresa's concern about "others" controlling her finances and Emily's health influence social work interventions with her?

3. In groups of two or three, arrange to visit a city/county health facility that serves small children. Ask about the process of obtaining a Medicaid card, making an appointment for a sick child, and other services offered by the clinic. Note the condition of the facility, the atmosphere and general helpfulness of staff to clients, and accessibility of services for clients. Report back to class the following week, including recommendations for Teresa's worker and for the clinic to ensure that Emily is well served.

4. Search the Internet for information on acute myelogenous leukemia. What are its distinguishing features, prognosis, and symptoms? What are the latest treatments and their impact on the patient and family? What is the life expectancy of a child with the disease?

References and Recommended Reading

Queralt, M. (1996) Latino families. In *The social environment and human behavior: A diversity perspective* (pp.401-441). Needham Heights, MA: Allyn and Bacon.

Shapiro, E. R. (1994). Family systems theory and models of family bereavement. In *Grief as a family process* (125-140). New York: Guilford.

Under the Table

The Agency

The agency is a public elementary school and you are the campus-based social worker who provides support services for students, families, staff and the neighborhood. The school population reflects a largely African-American and Hispanic community. The school staff is mostly composed of white females. On this campus, the following specialized programs are offered: special education, early childhood, and behavior management classes.

The Client System

Joseph (age 8) is an African-American student in the second grade, who was orphaned last year when his mother died of AIDS. Joseph's mother was drug addicted and had been in and out of several treatment programs and corrections facilities since Joseph was four. During her absences, Joseph and his teenage brother were cared for by their maternal grandmother. However, this grandparent died six months prior to Joseph's mother. His only remaining relatives are two aunts who each agreed to care for one of the boys. This arrangement took Joseph to a new state, new family, and new school, and separated him from his sibling.

Joseph currently lives with his Aunt Jo, Uncle Lou and their three sons (ages five, twelve, and seventeen). Uncle Lou, recently retired from the military, has expressed resentment over his wife's decision to care for Joseph. The family does not have formal guardianship of Joseph at this time.

Joseph is an extremely quiet child, usually answering questions in monosyllables. He appears to be small for his age and shows some physical characteristics of fetal alcohol syndrome. He cries easily and seems hungry all of the time, begging for leftover food in the cafeteria from students and staff. Uncle Lou is requiring Joseph to participate in physical training exercises with his sons (e.g., push-ups, running, chin-ups) under his supervision. He refers to Joseph as a "weenie" in comparison to the cousins.

In school, Joseph struggles with basic reading skills and finds school tasks to be very difficult and frustrating. Teachers describe his behavior as "off task, inattentive and withdrawn." He seems to avoid any interactions with peers, preferring to wander alone on the edge of the playground. In the classroom, the teacher will often find him under a desk or table playing with small items.

Special Issues

Establishing rapport and trust with this family may offer some special challenges for the social worker. It is important to consider the impact and relevance of the many adjustment issues in this case, including unresolved grief, loss, separation and neglect, developmental delays, and special education needs. Family support and effective parenting skills for use with Joseph need consideration. Issues of culturally competent practice are also important.

Key Concepts and Principles

Protective Factors

Individual characteristics that facilitate resiliency (Henderson, 1996). Identification of protective factors will assist in the initial assessment of this case and will aid in the establishment of rapport with both Joseph and his family.

Suggested Activities

1. Role play an individual session between the school social worker and Joseph using non-directive play therapy techniques.

2. Develop a strengths/assets list along with a clear statement of prioritized presenting problems.

3. Construct an eco-map and genogram compiling both systems and family relationship information to complete the mezzo and macro assessment.

4. Role play a staffing of this student by school personnel, with the social worker facilitating.

5. Research community resources for this family.

6. Practice teaching the communication skill of "I" messages to Joseph's guardians.

7. Research legislation in your state regarding the establishment of social services in school systems, particularly school social workers. How has policy affected the delivery of social services in your community?

References and Recommended Reading

Ewalt, P. L., Freeman, E. M., Kirk, S. A., & Poole, D. L. (1997). *Multicultural issues in social work.* Washington DC: NASW Press.

Henderson, N., & Milstein, M. M. (1996). *Resiliency in schools: Making it happen for students and educators.* Thousand Oaks, CA: Corwin.

Morrow, G. (1987). *The compassionate school: A practical guide to educating abused and traumatized children.* Englewood Cliffs, NJ: Prentice-Hall.

Shulman, L. (1999). *The skills of helping individuals, families, groups and communities.* Itasca, IL: F. E. Peacock.

Chapter 2

Interpreting Roles Within the Agency Context

A variety of social work roles and activities, including collaboration with other professionals and institutions, are often needed to work effectively with clients.

You Can't Go Home Again

The Agency

The agency is a large public psychiatric hospital which has a special unit for treating children and adolescents. Staff consist of two full-time social workers, a psychiatrist who serves as director of the unit and does very little direct treatment, several psychiatric nurses, and dorm staff who function somewhat as house parents. The facility is funded by state taxes and is well maintained, but "extras" are supplied by volunteer time and donations. The philosophy of treatment is dictated by the medical model, but innovative approaches to treatment are encouraged and the unit has the reputation of being a good training facility for emerging professional therapists across several disciplines.

The Client System

Dawn (age 11) is an attractive, well-groomed white girl with long brown hair and lovely green eyes. She has large red bumps on her face and scars on her arms. She seems to be nervous, frequently laughing inappropriately, talking rapidly, and jumping from subject to subject.

Dawn was admitted to the children's unit from a private psychiatric hospital after her insurance no longer covered her stay there. She was hospitalized after expressing suicidal ideation, cutting herself with several objects, eating glass, and tying her fingers with string until they turned blue. Dawn was sexually abused by her stepfather when she was five and six. He confessed and received a probated sentence. Dawn's mother still has a relationship with him. Dawn's older brother also admitted to forcing Dawn to perform oral sex with him and his friends. Child Protective Services is investigating, and it is likely that parental rights will be terminated. You have been assigned to work with Dawn in the role of therapist, a role distinct in this setting from family therapist or case manager, focused only on the work of individual therapy. At the time you were assigned to work with Dawn, she had been on the unit for one week. Staff is concerned that she fabricates stories for attention, and they hope that with individual therapy two times a week she will receive some of the positive adult attention that she seems to crave. Dawn's anticipated length of stay is uncertain, dependent on her progress and the availability of a safe environment upon discharge.

Special Issues

There is disagreement as to whether the therapist role should be separated from the case manager role as it is in this setting. In separating the two functions, the therapy role is "pure" and the relationship can be more clearly focused on the work of therapy without distractions. A disadvantage lies in the very strength of the model. By separating the role of therapist from other professional roles in the setting, the worker may not have a clear perception of the family and life context of the child. He or she must rely on the input from other staff to fill in the "big picture."

Defining the role of the worker and the client and the purpose of their work together is a significant aspect of beginning any professional relationship. Even for a child who has been in treatment before, no two therapists are alike, and one cannot assume that just because the child knows the word "therapist," that means he/she understands anything about how you will work together.

Managing one's own feelings in dealing with a child who has been so badly mistreated is among the most difficult challenges in the professional life of a social worker. When the caseload consists only of children who have been abused and neglected there is frequently a very high turnover in staff. It is very important for workers to be aware of the effects of working with abused children and build in, through supervision and peer support, some constructive outlets for expressing the anger and sadness that is a natural part of witnessing the trauma experienced by abused children.

Key Concepts and Principles

Secondary traumatization
> The process whereby a worker is negatively affected by hearing or bearing witness to horrific client experiences. The amount of stress varies from worker to worker, but it is generally accepted that a cumulative effect occurs as workers listen to clients' experiences.

Case management
> The coordination of a number of different resources on behalf of clients through a variety of professional roles.

Suggested Activities

1. Illustrate through role play how you would define your role and discuss the limits of your time together.

2. Identify three nonverbal activities that could assist this client to express her feelings. How would you go about deciding which activity to use and why?

3. Discuss what should be included in a treatment plan and why. What are the major components? Develop a form that would solicit the information you believe would be essential for any treatment plan.

4. Learn about the availability of therapeutic foster homes in your area and how foster parents are selected. Compare and contrast private and public therapeutic foster care agency policies.

References and Recommended Reading

Canino, I. A., & Spurlock, J. (1994). *Culturally diverse children and adolescents.* New York: Guilford.

Gil, E. (1991). *The healing power of play.* New York: Guilford.

Lukas, S. (1993). *Where to start and what to ask: An assessment handbook.* New York: Norton.

The Many Faces of Marsha

The Agency

Louis Elementary is located in an established neighborhood and serves students from prekindergarten through fifth grade. Forty-six percent of the school population is "at risk" according to state guidelines for determining "at risk" status (i.e., free and reduced meals, failed one or more section of the state examination [grades 3-5], an open and ongoing case with child protective services for abuse or neglect, retained in the last year, scored one to two years below chronological age on a kindergarten assessment test, or identified as having limited English proficiency on a language assessment). Louis Elementary has a special education population of 21% who are not included in the "at risk" population because their academic needs are met by an alternative program.

You are a school social worker who provides comprehensive support services to students, staff and families. Services include individual and group counseling as well as several preventative and supportive programs.

The Client System

Marsha (age 38) is a white female who has two children attending the school. Mandy is seven years old and is in the second grade. Danny (age 10) is in the fifth grade—currently placed in an "alternate classroom" through Special Education. Danny has a diagnosis of Oppositional Disorder with characteristics of Attention-Deficit Hyperactivity Disorder, and learning disorders in math and reading. Mandy is in a regular class setting.

Marsha also has two teenage daughters, Tina (age 14) and Tammy (age 18), who live at home but do not attend school. Tina is home-schooled by Marsha, and Tammy is employed at the local mall. Marsha has been married to Tom for 19 years, and the family moved from another state to your area several years ago.

Marsha has asked the school's social worker to meet with her after a recent Admission/Review/Dismissal meeting on Danny. You have an ongoing relationship with this family, mostly acting as a liaison between the family and school regarding Danny's behavioral issues. Recently, both of the children's teachers have voiced concerns about the children's erratic and inconsistent attitudes and behaviors. In addition, both teachers have consulted with you about Marsha, who seems to have "strange and unpredictable mood patterns" at school and on the phone with school personnel.

Marsha recently received several phone calls and notes from her children's teachers about concerns. Marsha begins her session with you by expressing nervousness and apprehension over "what I need to tell you." Marsha reveals that she is diagnosed as having Dissociative Identity Disorder (DID) and is currently in therapy several times per week. She indicates that through counseling she and her therapist have identified five distinctly different personalities: a three-year- old, a five-year-old, a twelve-year-old, an eighteen-year-old and a "narrator" who can act as an interpreter among all of the personalities. Marsha also reveals that she was hospitalized for a suicide attempt last year and was in a follow-up group for several months. Her current therapist is one of the facilitators from that group. Due to the (DID) Marsha is unable to hold a job and has no insurance coverage. She has applied for Supplemental Security Income (SSI) benefits. Her therapist provides pro bono sessions at this time, and is assisting her with the SSI application process.

Marsha indicates that she probably has "been out" as one of her other personalities, sometimes at school while picking up or dropping off the children or volunteering. Therefore, Marsha is not surprised that the staff is confused about her as well as about the children's behaviors. She asks you to assist her with the children's issues during this time of turmoil. The therapist has sent a business card with Marsha, and indicates a willingness to collaborate.

Special Issues

Issues include identifying the scope of the work of a school social worker in this situation. Confidentiality issues must be considered. Working with a client who is involved in counseling elsewhere may present issues of treatment boundaries. Knowledge of DID is important.

Key Concepts and Principles

Social work in a host setting

The provision of social work services in agencies or organizations primarily dedicated to a different purpose. In a school setting, the social worker may be a part of a community social service agency that is contracted to provide in-school services.

Suggested Activities

1. Role play a session with the social worker, the therapist, and Marsha.
2. Discuss possible ethical dilemmas to be considered.
3. Develop eco-maps detailing the overlapping systems, stressors and sources of strength.
4. Research DID.
5. Discuss micro, mezzo, and macro issues from the perspective of the social worker's supervisor.
6. Develop a prioritized list of case management issues.
7. Role play a session with the social worker, the two teachers, the therapist, and Marsha.
8. Have a class discussion around aspects of this case that are uncomfortable.
9. Discuss strategies for interventions with each client system.

References and Recommended Reading

Dudley, C. D. (1997). *Treating depressed children: A therapeutic manual of cognitive behavioral interventions*, Oakland, CA: New Harbinger.

Kirst-Ashman, K. K., & Hull, G. H., (1999). *Understanding generalist practice* (2nd ed.). Chicago, IL: Nelson-Hall.

Wachtel, E. T. (1994). *Troubled children and their families*. New York: Guilford.

Chapter 3

Collecting Data

Data collection is the ongoing exploration of facts and contexts related to the presenting problem, client strengths, client needs, people involved, and the values underlying various options for problem solving.

Homeless

The Agency

At AIDS Assistance Inc., you are an intake worker in charge of addressing needs and requests by phone and by "walk-ins." Most clients have an HIV positive diagnosis from the public clinic that does testing. The agency is new and small but is already providing intake, information and referral services, public education, and a food pantry for those clients whose income does not allow for adequate nutrition. Other services are provided by existing agencies.

The local hospice program addresses basic income and emergency housing, as well as palliative care for those clients who are reaching the end stage of the disease. Collaboration with two hospitals handles the majority of the uninsured clients needing acute care. Pharmaceutical services are accessed through a network of providers and local drug stores. Approximately 50 volunteers assist with transportation for clients who are too ill to drive or use public transportation for medical appointments. After intake, clients remain as active or inactive cases until their deaths. There are eight case managers who share a caseload of 150–200 clients in the metroplex.

The Client System

Miss Agnes (age 20) is an African-American female diagnosed as HIV positive. She arrived as a walk-in client. Within the first few minutes of her arrival, it became clear that Miss Agnes had been homeless for several years and in ill health during the last six to eight months. Although she tested negative a year ago, Miss Agnes suspected she would now test positive due to use of a "dirty" needle, and infection from an on-and-off boyfriend who disappeared about nine months ago. Miss Agnes looks neat but frail, and appears downcast. She carries an old leather backpack out of which she takes some documents, thus revealing a collection of shoes, shirts and an umbrella. Background information reveals that Miss Agnes recently attended a junior college in her hometown, but that her immediate plans do not include continuation of her education. She volunteers little about her family of origin—only that her parents are very busy with their careers. She wears gold-rimmed glasses that make her look scholarly, a colorful turban, and no jewelry. When asked about her breakfast, Miss Agnes mumbled that she saved some of her dinner from the previous night and will eat it as soon as she gets hungry. You have obtained all of this information at the intake interview.

Special Issues

Persons who are homeless share many survival needs. However, they must be individualized according to the current situations, their backgrounds and their aspirations. Connecting quickly with these clients and contracting with them explicitly is particularly critical since they may be unavailable for follow-up service by agency staff.

Key Concepts and Principles

Empathic listening
> A style of listening in which the social worker perceives the experience of the client without judgment.

Strengths perspective
>An approach used in assessment and planning to guide mutual problem-solving based on resources and potential abilities that the client may have, but may not be utilizing in the midst of a problematic situation.

Self-determination
>To allow the client to make choices for problem resolution or goal attainment.

Suggested Activities

1. Role-play the initial interview with an emphasis on data collection.

2. Reflect on and discuss the following. How can the social worker communicate interest in the client's well-being? What might appear as judgmental? What information is needed prior to problem solving? What is the difference between an initial contract and one developed with a client who has accepted services?

3. Role-play Session #2: Assume Miss Agnes agrees to be an agency client. Part of an initial contract includes her agreement to meet with a group of other clients who are homeless and HIV-positive. How would the social worker introduce the purpose of the group to these clients? Role play the first group session. Follow-up with a discussion of how the group context helped or hindered the individuals' problem-solving.

4. Explore social policy issues for people diagnosed as being HIV positive. If these people are to have adequate and accessible care, what services does you community need to provide? What relevant policies are in place in class members' field placement agencies?

References and Recommended Reading

Evans, D. R., Hearn, M. T., Uhlemann, M. R., & Ivey, A. E. (1998). *Essential interviewing: A programmed approach to effective communication* (5th ed.). Pacific Grove, CA: Brooks/Cole.

Hepworth, D. H., Rooney, R. H., & Larsen, J. A. (1997). *Direct social work practice: Theory and skills* (5th ed.). Pacific Grove, CA: Brooks/ Cole.

Shulman, L. (1992). *The skills of helping individuals, families, and groups.* Itasca, IL: F. E. Peacock.

Toseland, R. W., & Rivas, R. F. (1998). *An introduction to group work practice* (3rd ed.). Needham Heights, MA: Allyn and Bacon.

New Beginnings—Part I

The Agency

New Beginnings is a community mental health clinic with 50 staff members offering individual, family, couples, and group treatment for children, adolescents, and adults. The agency has a sliding fee scale. Agency workers come from a variety of professional backgrounds and are prepared to assist clients experiencing depression, anxiety disorders, posttraumatic stress disorder, and other mental health concerns. You are one of several social workers providing treatment.

The Client System

Margaret Hernandez (age 38), an attractive, Hispanic homemaker, is seeking services from New Beginnings. Margaret tells you that about a year ago, during an early evening jog on a local running and biking trail, she was raped by a male acquaintance from her gym. The man, also a runner, joined her for the last part of her run, then forced her into his truck at the parking lot. He threatened to hurt her if she ever told her husband what had happened. If she did tell, he would tell her husband that it was consensual sex. Frightened, Margaret believed him and told herself that she "would just forget about the whole thing."

Soon after the rape, Margaret had flashbacks and nightmares and wondered if she was "going crazy." She also began to experience physical symptoms—racing heart, a choking sensation, feeling faint, shaking hands, intense fear of dying—and began to spend more and more time at home. Additionally, she feels depressed, doesn't sleep well or eat much, and is irritable much of the time. She

quit running, which was her primary mode of stress management. The only outside activity she feels comfortable doing is attending Sunday Mass with her family.

Margaret states that she feels overwhelmed by her usual responsibilities. Lisa (age 15) and Juan (age 13) are capable of caring for themselves and helping around the house, but prefer to hang out with their friends and be involved in sports and other extracurricular activities. Her youngest son, David (age 9), has Down's Syndrome and needs assistance in self-care and day-to-day activities.

Margaret's husband, Paul (age 42) is an architect who works long hours and, when home, does little to help out with the housework or children. Margaret says she frequently nags at him about his drinking, to which he answers "I don't have a problem." His drinking is upsetting to her because her father is an alcoholic. Since the assault, Margaret's marriage has been suffering. She finds sex terrifying, but can't tell Paul why. Instead, she makes up excuses. Paul senses this change in her, begins to accuse her of being cold and uncaring, and insists upon sexual relations, stating "it's my right as a husband."

Margaret thought that she had put most of the sexual assault behind her. However, she no longer enjoys sexual intimacy, doesn't understand why she feels depressed and anxious, and fears that her life is falling apart.

Special Issues

Anyone working with Margaret will need to be sensitive to the roles that the Hispanic culture and Roman Catholicism may have in this situation. More traditional Hispanic communities may teach both males and females that a woman who is raped may have "sinned" or somehow "encouraged" the perpetrator.

In addition to the sexual assault, Margaret faces a number of other issues: parenting adolescents and a Down's Syndrome child, depression and anxiety, and a spouse who is somewhat disconnected and possibly abusing alcohol.

Key Concepts and Principles

Cultural competency

The necessity for a social worker to be knowledgeable about differing needs and values among diverse clients, including how to work with clients regarding specific ethnic and acculturation issues.

Strengths approach

Social workers assessing for and calling attention to what is going well, (i.e., what positives there are in the client and client's situation) rather than focusing only on problems or troubles.

Posttraumatic stress

An intense reaction to a traumatic event that involves cognitive, emotional, and physical symptoms.

Suggested Activities

1. In small groups, discuss the most pertinent areas of data collection relating to Margaret's case and list the client's strengths.

2. Discuss community services, social service agencies, and legal services that could potentially be involved in working with Margaret. Prioritize services most helpful for Margaret's situation.

3. Invite a speaker from a local rape crisis center to speak about rape and the legal system, common reactions to rape, and how to help those who have been sexually assaulted.

4. Role play a meeting between the social worker and the couple in which Margaret wants to disclose the assault to her husband during the session.

5. Discuss societal perceptions of violence against women. Have students identify personal biases related to this topic.

References and Recommended Reading

Herman, J. (1997). *Trauma and recovery: The aftermath of violence—from domestic abuse to political terror.* New York: Basic Books.

Ledray, L. E. (1994). *Recovering from rape.* New York: Henry Holt and Company.

Matsakis, A. (1994). *Post-traumatic stress disorder: A complete treatment guide.* Oakland, CA: New Harbinger.

McGoldrick, M., Giordano, J., & Pearce, J. K. (1996). *Ethnicity and family therapy* (2nd ed.). New York: Guilford.

All in the Family—Part I

The Agency

The Sprucewood Mental Health Center is a state-run agency serving individuals and families of all ages. The center has a special program that focuses on the needs and problems of adolescents. The teen program offers individual treatment, as well as support groups for males and females. As a social worker in the teen program, you provide individual treatment and make referrals to support groups and to other workers.

The Client System

Jessica Smith (age 15) is an attractive, white high school sophomore. She reports that she is happy with the way her second year of high school is going. She is a slim and athletic junior varsity cheerleader, who is popular among her peers, brings home good grades and is beginning to date.

Jessica is not overweight, yet she is worried that she does not look as good in her cheerleading uniform as her friend, Sandra, who recently lost some weight and in Jessica's opinion, looks fabulous. Sandra disclosed to Jessica that she vomits when she eats too much, and this helps her to maintain her weight. Jessica decided to engage in the same behavior, and had done so for about a month when her mother discovered her in the bathroom one evening. Alarmed, her mother placed a call the next day to a social worker. Jessica "can't understand what the fuss is about," and is angry about having to meet with a social worker. She imagines that she "will be the talk of the school." Jessica believes that her mother is pinning all of her hopes on her since her brother decided against attending college. Jessica wishes she "would just leave me alone."

Jessica's father, James, has an engineering job at a large computer corporation, is not home much, and when he is, keeps to himself. According to Jessica, this is alright with her, and she says she has "a hard time relating to my intellectual, introspective father." Jessica also confesses that she thinks he tends to drink beer on the weekends, and then becomes more talkative and argumentative. To escape the arguments, Jessica says she and her sister, Millie (age 8), leave the house and take the family dog for a walk.

Special Issues

Bulimia and anorexia are among the fastest growing disorders of today's adolescent females. These disorders are complicated to treat due to the pervasiveness of thin women in the media. Data collection with adolescent females experiencing eating disorders may be difficult to accomplish since many females with eating disorders frequently deny that their eating habits are problematic and may not wish to share any details.

Key Concepts and Principles

Developmental stage—adolescence
> The period of time between 12 and 18 years, in which physical and cognitive maturation, emotional development, and relationship and identity exploration occur.

Eating disorders

> Severe disturbances in eating behavior that are accompanied by distorted perceptions of body shape and weight. Anorexia is characterized by a refusal to maintain a minimally normal body weight, and bulimia is defined by repeated binge eating and purging.

Mother-daughter relationships

> A core relationship in the lives of women that can serve as a model for relating to others and self, as well as empathic development. It is marked by periods of pleasure, conflict, separation, and mutual growth.

Suggested Activities

1. Discuss how social workers might gather information during interviews with clients who are not interested in sharing personal details or don't see their behaviors as problematic.

2. Invite a social worker who treats eating disorders to talk with the class.

3. Discuss societal beliefs and norms that contribute to the low self-esteem of our nation's teenage girls. Once the beliefs/norms are identified, discuss ways social workers can help to reduce these pressures on teenagers.

4. Role play the Smith family with two students as social workers, and other students playing the roles of each family member. In the role play, the social workers attempt to help the family understand how the current dynamics are contributing to Jessica's eating disorder. The workers may decide to continue working with the whole family, or work with different groupings of family members.

5. In small groups, create a support group for teen girls. Include topics that they would want to see addressed, activities that would be beneficial for teenage girls, etc. Each group presents their "proposal" to the class.

6. Invite adolescent girls to be in a panel discussion on the difficulties of peer relationships and social belonging in the school setting.

References and Recommended Reading

Gilligan, C. (1982). *In a different voice: Psychological theory and women's development.* Cambridge, MA: Harvard University Press.

Jordan, J. V., Kaplan, A. G., Miller, J. B., Stuver, I. P., & Surrey, J. L. (1991). *Women's growth in connection: Writings from the stone center.* New York: Guilford.

Lukas, S. (1993). *Where to start and what to ask: An assessment handbook.* New York: Norton.

Pipher, M. B. (1994). *Reviving Ophelia: Saving the selves of adolescent girls.* New York: Ballantine.

Wolf, N. (1991). *The beauty myth: How images of beauty are used against women.* New York: Doubleday.

Chapter 4

Defining the Problem

Problem definition is a process by which the client and social worker share the reason for the professional contact including needs and related issues.

Platica

The Agency

The Children's Rehabilitation Center is a multiservice, nonprofit, interdisciplinary organization funded through Easter Seals, United Way, private insurance, and special grants. You are a social worker responsible for intake and initiating the comprehensive evaluation process with the families, scheduling all the various specialist services, and leading the interdisciplinary staffing on each referred child.

The Client System

Anita Martinez (age 23), who speaks limited English, was referred by a pediatric clinic to the Children's Rehabilitation Center to ask for information which may help her and her family in caring for Ricardo (age 2) who is still unable to walk. Due to Ricardo's size and weight, the concern is for Mrs. Martinez' health as well as Ricardo's well being. Currently, he is approximately 12 pounds over the desired weight. Mrs. Martinez, who has to carry Ricardo much of the time, is finding this task increasingly difficult. She is also finding it difficult to bathe him. The pediatrician recommends surgery for Ricardo, which will require the child to wear specially ordered footwear for several years. Mrs. Martinez and her husband Manuel (age 23), a day laborer, cannot afford surgery or special shoes and have requested assistance from the center. Mrs. Martinez and Manuel have been married for seven years and have three other children: Carmen (age 6 1/2), Guillermo "Memo," (age 5), and Jose "Paco," (age 3 1/2). All three older siblings are without disabilities.

Ricardo appears to be a cheerful child. Although he uses his arms to pull himself to his favorite toys, he likes to be carried by his older siblings, his father and Mrs. Martinez, as well as the other extended family members who frequent their home and volunteer to help out. Concern is focused on Mrs. Martinez because she recently sprained her back trying to lift Ricardo out of the bathtub. During her recuperation, Mr. Martinez would place Ricardo in a playpen where he had access to his toys and some snacks. During school and work hours, no one was around to help Mrs. Martinez keep up with Ricardo's needs. The paternal grandmother used her lunch break to change Ricardo and make sure he and Mrs. Martinez had everything they needed for the afternoon. The family is very concerned about how Ricardo's condition could further cause health problems for Mrs. Martinez and thus endanger her caregiving for what is already a rather large family with small children. You, as the intake worker, have obtained all of this information and have determined that they are eligible for services.

Special Issues

A number of issues have considerable impact on the family: limited use of English by the mother, developmental disabilities, medical needs, and financial limitations.

Key Concepts and Principles

Cultural diversity

Differences within and among client systems often include various values, customs, and preferences that are attributable to their ethnic or familial origins. The social worker must avoid stereotypical assumptions and at the same time be alert to the uniqueness of the individual.

Developmental disabilities

Physical and mental impairments to optimal development that appear before the age of 22 and that present specific challenges throughout life. These impairments may affect a person's daily life and level of independence.

Suggested Activities

1. Role play the first contact with Mrs. Martinez. (Questions to consider: How does the worker communicate interest and respect to Mrs. Martinez until the interpreter is ready to assist? How does the worker ask Mrs. Martinez for permission to bring in someone else to interpret?)

2. Role play Session #2: Mr. Martinez has joined his wife for this session. Proceed to define the problem as well as review the previously acquired data, obtain more input from the father, and continue to gather information on Ricardo's developmental history, the care that he requires, how various members of the family have participated, and what their greatest concerns are at this time. Provide them the option to continue the process within the agency or to delay or cancel their request for assistance. Are there other options available to this family?

3. Discuss the use of interpreters. How is the interpreter introduced to the client? Keep in mind that in Spanish a literal translation of discussion could be interpreted by clients as confrontational rather than a two-way conversation about their needs and preferences. Therefore it is best to prepare clients for a "platica" (a conversation) related to their situation.

4. Discuss the potential benefits and risks of making a home visit.

5. Eco-mapping: Develop an eco-map to depict the Martinez family in the context of the extended family, their culture-based support systems, and the available community resources.

6. Role-play Session #3: Assign various interdisciplinary roles and functions to five or six members of the class group and simulate a staffing in which the social worker presents the information about the Martinez situation. Then, use the interdisciplinary team to discuss how the evaluation/assessment of the Martinez situation will proceed.

7. In small groups, add a culturagram to the eco-map to illustrate the Martinez family's situation. Discuss how you could use the culturagram to explore Mrs. Martinez' recent immigration and the implications of this cultural factor on how the family can prepare for long-term caregiving.

References and Recommended Reading

Congress, E. P. (1994). The use of culturagrams to assess and empower culturally diverse families. *Families in Society, 75,* 531-540.

Hepworth, D. H., Rooney, R. H., & Larsen, J. A. (1997). *Direct social work practice: Theory and skills* (5th ed.). Pacific Grove, CA: Brooks/Cole.

Mary, N. L. (1998). Social work and the support model of services for people with developmental disabilities. *Social Work Education, 34,* 247-260.

McBride, S. L., & Brotherson, M. J. (1997). Guiding practitioners toward valuing and implementing family-centered practices. In P. J. Winton, J. A. McCollum, & C. Catlett (Eds.), *Reforming personnel preparation in early intervention: Issues, models and practical strategies* (pp. 253-276). Baltimore, MD: Paul H. Brookes.

Sheafor, B. W., Horejsi, C. R., & Horejsi, G. A. (1997). *Techniques and guidelines for social work practice* (4th ed.). Needham Heights, MA: Allyn and Bacon.

Street Kid

The Agency

The family therapy center within the neighborhood medical clinic evolved from the desire of the physicians who treated patients in the clinic to have access to counseling in the same convenient location. Planners recognized that patients who trust their doctors in the clinic would be more likely to follow through on counseling referrals especially if those resources were made available under one roof. The private, nonprofit clinic is managed by a religious charity and serves the working class poor on a sliding fee basis. They are primarily Hispanics, with a smaller percentage of white and African-American clients. The family therapy center is under the direction of the clinic director, a physician, but the center has its own administrator who is a clinical social worker and who also maintains a caseload of clients. One other part time social worker is on staff.

The Client System

Shanda (age 17) is an African-American female referred for counseling from the medical clinic. Prior to this referral, Shanda had been diagnosed with several benign tumors on her arms and back that were successfully removed surgically. Shanda is on probation for assaultive behavior and admits being a member of a local African-American youth gang. The judge suggested Shanda's behavior was related to anxiety over her medical condition, and mandated that she see a therapist.

Shanda's immediate family includes her mother, a younger brother, and a father who lives in another city and whom she rarely sees. Her parents are not legally divorced, but have not lived together for several years. After the initial session, Shanda seemed to open up more when her mother was not present, and while not spontaneous, she did answer questions freely. Shanda denied she had any concerns about her medical condition, and expressed that her only goal was to get off probation. She admitted that she was involved in "lots of fights," the last one with a school official who she thought was going to undress her to search for drugs. This episode was the primary reason she was placed on probation.

Shanda never acknowledged that fighting or aggressive behavior was a problem. For her, fighting was surviving in the world she had grown up in, and she was adamant that she had done nothing wrong since she only fought when people "messed" with her. Her probation officer wanted Shanda to work on several goals during therapy: self-presentation and dress, use of birth control, taking responsibility for her actions, and discussing her feelings about her medical condition.

Special Issues

Finding a common ground between the referring party and a non-voluntary client is sometimes very challenging. Shanda's mother and her probation officer see problems for which Shanda is not motivated to work. Some common mistakes in situations like this include the worker being too eager to move into problem solving without sufficient exploration, assuming that the referral problem is the problem-to-be-worked, and not starting where the client is.

Another issue is working with involuntary clients. Discovering what the client is motivated to do or be and finding creative ways to acknowledge and align with them is an initial challenge.

Also, white, middle-class models for anger management may sound hollow, silly, or even dangerous to any client whose daily life is filled with violence. Peer counseling may be more effective than individual counseling in this aspect of working with street kids.

Key Concepts and Principles

Self-determination

All clients have choices. Helping clients identify the choices they do have can be a very effective intervention. Involuntary clients, by definition, come to agencies believing they do not have a choice or that the alternatives make their ability not to choose social services only theoretical. When workers acknowledge client feelings about being pressured or coerced, and invite them to participate in planning their time together, clients become less defensive and more empowered to choose within the externally imposed constraints.

Resistance

Resistance is a self-protective, conscious, or unconscious response to a perceived threat. Most people resist change to some degree, even when the change is welcomed, because every change means some loss of what is familiar and comfortable. When resistance is met with respect and empathy, clients have an opportunity to become more open and engaged in the helping process.

Suggested Activities

1. Identify ways you, as a social worker, would begin to establish rapport with Shanda and explore her view of the situation.

2. Interview a police officer from a neighborhood known for gang activity or invite a panel of individuals who have experience working with gangs. What current policies guide the police in working with gangs in your city? How are the police connected with other agencies?

3. Role play the issue of confidentiality with this client. How does it differ from a voluntary client?

4. Role play an interview with a probation officer regarding the officer's expectations and goals for Shanda. Clarify the resources and limits of the services offered through the agency.

References and Recommended Reading

Cournoyer, B. (1996). *The social work skills workbook.* (2nd ed.). Pacific Grove: Brooks/Cole.

Leigh, J. W. (1998). *Communicating for cultural competence.* Needham Heights, MA: Allyn and Bacon.

Wing Sue, D., & Sue, D. (1990). *Counseling the culturally different: Theory and practice.* (2nd ed.). New York: Wiley.

Chapter 5

Initial Assessment/ Identifying Strengths

Assessment involves the process of determining the nature, cause, progression, and prognosis of a problem and the personalities and situations involved therein (Barker, 1999).

In identifying strengths, workers also call attention to what is going well (i.e., what positives there are in the client and client's situation), rather than focusing only on problems or troubles.

La Migra

The Agency

You are a social worker in a private, nonprofit organization designed to address the needs of immigrants. Most of the clientele are from Mexico and Central America. The staff includes two social workers, the director and other office personnel, and three part-time volunteers who are bilingual. A retired attorney helps with referrals to lawyers who can do pro bono work when immigrants need assistance with matters such as the legal immigration process or claims for injuries on the job. There is also a very well liked receptionist who has been with the agency for the last nine years. The latter speaks enough Spanish to communicate basic greetings and agency information sought by new clientele.

The Client System

Mrs. Fernandez (age 35), a frequent service recipient, arrives to ask for assistance with her two daughters: (Oralia, age 13, and Mari, age 14). Oralia was escorted home by a police officer after she was found violating curfew hours at a nearby park last night. Mrs. Fernandez complained rather strongly that it is hard enough to be adapting to life without her husband without having the constant bickering between her two daughters. Oralia was alone at the park following a heated argument with her sister. Mrs. Fernandez, fortunately, had just arrived home from her second job when the officer arrived with Oralia; otherwise, she stated "no telling what might have happened." Both girls attend the same intermediate school and do fairly well. Mrs. Fernandez just accepted a second job (janitorial work in an office building) and is therefore out of the house from 6:30AM to 11:00PM. By the time she returns from work, she expects the girls to have fed themselves, prepared school work and clothes for the next day and run any errands necessary for the upkeep of their home. Mrs. Fernandez and the girls ride buses to work and school respectively.

The Fernandez family has experienced financial difficulties before, but their situation worsened after Mr. Fernandez was deported to Mexico some three months ago. He was picked up by "La Migra" (Immigration and Naturalization Service officers) while working at a nearby construction site. Now, not only are they having to support themselves, they want to save a little each month to help him try to get back to the United States. He has found some part-time employment in a border town and is also trying to save enough money to get home. An additional challenge they face is that of sending a few dollars for the upkeep of their older daughters who stayed in Mexico.

As you gather information about the family, you learn that they have no other relatives in the community. Two older daughters, ages 15 and 16, remained behind with their maternal grandmother in the southwestern region of Mexico. There are no immediate plans for them to join the rest of the family. Mrs. Fernandez and the younger girls moved north seven years ago, to join Mr. Fernandez. The couple is very proud of the progress of all four girls, and their dream is that each two sets of daughters can prosper in their respective living sites. Both Mr. and Mrs. Fernandez finished primary school (6th grade) prior to getting married. They were both attending an English class prior to his deportation. The family has visited a Pentecostal church in the neighborhood but is undecided about joining. It was the church pastor who suggested that Mrs. Fernandez take her daughters for counseling. Mrs. Fernandez first confirmed that the agency would not inquire about her immigration status or that of the girls.

Mrs. Fernandez agreed to obtain outside help because she feels unable to control the situation. Also, she has begun to get severe headaches, to the point of asking around to see if there is a senora (folk healer also known as curandera). Meanwhile, she is drinking manzanilla (Chamomile) as an herbal medication.

Special Issues

Immigrant families experience separations. In addition to economic problems, these separations and the complications associated with trying to legalize immigration often create crisis conditions. Roles in the family system are often shifted to accommodate changes caused by deportation, reunification, or changes in employment.

Key Concepts and Principles

Microsystem
> Individual and family involved in the problem situation.

Mesosystem
> The small groups related to the individual or family microsystem. This may include extended family, neighbors and other natural support systems.

Macrosystem
> Large organizations and communities related to the microsystem.

Curanderismo
> An alternative health care system that offers a holistic approach to address physical and mental health concerns incorporating

cultural and spiritual aspects of the Mexican-American experience.

Suggested Activities

1. Role play the following interview interactions with Mrs. Fernandez:

a. Initial Interview—Develop an initial working relationship with Mrs. Fernandez by clarifying names used by the family and exploring natural support systems. Follow-up—Discuss how names provide data on family origins, level of acculturation and the parent's ability to individualize each child. Explore comfort level of an intern who is not Hispanic or is Hispanic but of a different background. Discuss how language preferences can be explored and how cultural competency is important in uncovering natural support systems (e.g., extended family and alternative health care systems, such as "la senora" who has provided teas and advice for Mrs. Fernandez and her family).

b. Role play a home visit—Introduce self and identify interview participants. Explore possible need for interpreter services. Explore family's well-being and family's strengths. Explore family's perspective on problem(s). Explore nature of community and its strengths. Explore family's use of alternative health care system. Follow-up—Discuss possible differences between an office based interview and a home visit. What are the advantages/disadvantages of each? What are interpreter services? What should be done when such services are not available and an interviewee does not speak English? Discuss ways to explore community and alternative health care systems as supports for the family.

2. Develop an eco-map for the scenario. Using a blank sheet of paper, draw a circle at the center of the page, then add two additional

circles around it. Label each of the three to correspond to person/family, the nurturing environment and the sustaining environment. Include all family members in the inner circle, adding brief notations as to names, ages, etc. On the next circle, add specific names of supportive individuals/groups and persons with whom the client system is interacting. In the outer circle add names of organizations or community groups representing the sustaining environment. Draw solid, broken, or wavy lines from persons in inner circle to systems in the outer circles to indicate supportive, needed, or conflicting relationships, respectively. Add to any of the circles those names of organizations/institutions which can potentially provide some resources, but which have not been accessed by the client system. Advanced level work: Include a genogram within the inner circle.

3. Discuss ways to recognize cultural clues in this scenario and use them for more effective intervention with Mrs. Fernandez.

4. Discuss how the principles of individualization, inclusion, and empowerment can be incorporated in work with this family.

5. Discuss the practitioner's responsibilities, self-determination of the client, and any ethical dilemmas that may emerge.

6. Discuss additional levels of intervention that could benefit this family and similar families. Then, identify the respective roles and functions social workers can use within the various levels of intervention in this situation.

7. Discuss Curanderismo as an alternative health care system used by some Hispanic families.

8. Visit a local hierberia, where traditional families obtain herbs that cannot be grown at home. Note the variety of candles and other religious items related to addressing the spiritual needs of families.

References and Recommended Reading

Barker, R. L. (1999). *The social work dictionary* (4th ed.). Washington, DC: NASW Press.

Kirst-Ashman, K. K., & Hull, H. H., Jr. (1999). *Understanding generalist practice* (2nd ed.). Chicago, IL: Nelson-Hall.

Sheafor, B. W., Horejsi, C. R., & Horejsi, G. A. (1997). *Techniques and guidelines for social work practice* (4th ed.). Needham Heights, MA: Allyn and Bacon.

Sporting Chance—Part I

The Agency

You are a social worker within a visiting teacher program in a local school district which includes approximately 60,000 students. Populations served are white, African-American, Hispanic, Asian, Native American, and refugees from Cuba, Central and South America, and the former Yugoslavia. The visiting teacher program includes personnel with professional experience as teachers, social workers, and counselors. Most of the work is referred by teachers and counselors, but any school employee can refer students whose behavior gives the appearance of personal or social problems. The visiting teacher gathers pertinent data regarding the situation from school personnel, the student, and the family system to ascertain problem areas and develop plans for intervention. School-based resources include school psychologists, special education specialists, and teachers, as well as various community-based services for children and youth. Most of the work involves group services, individual and family counseling, program development, and consultation for classroom teachers and school counselors.

The Client System

Victor Santos (age 15), a Hispanic male, is a high school freshman. He is lean, of average height and always looks healthy and neat. He is on the freshman baseball team and does relatively well in school. He speaks some Spanish as a second language. You are a social worker who has been meeting with Victor for about a month. He was referred to the visiting teacher program by his counselor after Victor's use of marijuana was reported by a school custodian. Victor insisted that it must have been someone else, and since there was no proof, Victor received no punishment. However, in the process of looking at the possible substance abuse issue, additional information from teachers and a baseball coach revealed that Victor had been seen associating with students who are known to be gang members and users of various drugs. Also, during the last six-week period, his grades dipped into low B and C levels, a distinct shift from his previous A and B performance. He also missed classes and baseball practice.

Victor lives alone with his mother in a small frame house several blocks from the school. Victor's father is serving a second prison term in an out-of-state federal prison for drug distribution. Victor has not seen his father since he was incarcerated five years ago. A preliminary telephone conference with Victor's mother indicated her concern about the situation and her support of intervention with her son.

During the last month, your conferences with Victor focused on regular attendance at school since he believes his low grades are due to missed work. He has no specific academic interests but wants to remain eligible to play baseball for the school.

Special Issues

Victor entered adolescence without a father in the home. Challenges associated with having a parent in prison are of particular importance now that Victor has begun to associate with peers who are allegedly using drugs.

Key Concepts and Principles

Client as expert

The use of the client's perspective regarding the problem, resources, and intervention options potentially available to resolve the problem.

Visiting teacher programs

Some school systems use a visiting teacher to assess students' emotional and behavioral issues. These staff may be certified teachers or social workers.

Children of incarcerated parents

Any child of the more than two million individuals in jails and state and federal prisons who may suffer separation and economic hardship that often goes unidentified.

Suggested Activities

1. Develop and discuss a list of strengths found in this scenario.

2. Role play a session between the worker and Victor to set attendance goals.

3. Role play a session with Mrs. Santos to address school problems. Explore and clarify issues of confidentiality.

4. Role play sessions with the worker and Victor to explore other possible problem areas.

5. Design a group program for students whose parents are in a correctional facility.

6. Role play a conference with a school administrator to obtain approval for your proposed group program for students with parents who are incarcerated.

7. Given administrative approval, discuss how to find students whose parents are incarcerated. What ethical dilemmas could be encountered? How can the students' privacy be safeguarded?

References and Recommended Reading

Hepworth, D. H., Rooney, R. H., & Larsen, J. A. (1997). *Direct social work practice: Theory and skills* (5th ed.). Pacific Grove, CA: Brooks/Cole.

Romo, H. D. (1996). *Latino high school graduation.* Austin, TX: University of Texas Press.

Sheafor, B. W., Horejsi, C. R., & Horejsi, G. A. (1994). *Techniques and guidelines for social work practice* (3rd. ed.). Needham Heights, MA: Allyn and Bacon.

Weick, A., & Saleebey, D. (1995). Supporting family strengths: Orienting policy and practice toward the 21st century. *Families in Society, 76,* 141-149.

Chapter 6

Contracting and Goal Setting

Contracting is the mutual process whereby worker and client develop and clarify expectations of each other, establish goals, and agree on the methods to accomplish these goals.

Goal setting is a skillful process to insure that goals are mutually agreed upon, realistic, and measurable.

The Power of Fear

The Agency

The Women's Shelter is a nonprofit agency serving women who are in need of protection from violent partners, and the children of these women. The agency is composed of a shelter for women without children and a family shelter with a wide array of counseling and support services (both individual and group) for women in the community who are not residing in the shelters. The agency prides itself on its outreach to ethnic minority communities and to young people through the teen dating violence program. You are new to the agency and have just completed your requisite orientation and training. Darlene is your first client in your new position.

The Client System

Darlene (age 29), a white female, first came to the Women's Shelter some years ago after having run away from a violent relationship in another state. She met and married her present husband a year later and almost immediately had two sons. Within five years, the domestic violence in that relationship forced her to again seek refuge in the shelter, at which time Darlene filed for divorce. Her husband convinced her he would change and wooed her back with gifts and promises to seek help. However, he subsequently intensified his harassment and eventually attempted to kill her. Narrowly escaping with her life, Darlene filed charges against him for attempted murder, and returned to the shelter with her two young sons. Darlene discloses to you that she was emancipated at the age of 16 to escape a violent family of origin where she and her mother were beaten regularly by an alcoholic father. Darlene has a history of anorexia as well as alcohol and drug abuse. She is currently attending Alcoholics Anonymous meetings and has been in recovery for two years.

Darlene declares that she is now determined to leave her husband permanently and break the cycle of violence for the sake of her children. She still does not know whether he will be sent to prison. She appears mentally, emotionally, and physically exhausted and has confided that she is tired of living in fear, but "fear is all I know."

Special Issues

Intervention for a client in crisis is concentrated on helping the client to rally her resources, both internal and external, as quickly as possible in order to facilitate return to her previous level of functioning, if not move beyond it to a more adaptive level. In this process the worker needs to be more directive to help the overwhelmed client partialize and prioritize concrete tasks and needs, and to offer concrete assistance in helping the client accomplish them. Assuring safety, food, shelter, and basic needs are of primary concern. For the worker to expect the client to engage in reflection about the cycle of abuse or counseling in a strict clinical sense at this time is unrealistic even if the client seems willing.

Key Concepts and Principles

Cycle of domestic violence
Domestic violence usually follows a predictably escalating pattern, increasing in

intensity over time without professional intervention. Denial is a key part of the cycle. Throughout the process both the batterer and partner deny the batterer's responsibility, the seriousness and danger of the battering, and that the violence will continue to occur.

Adult survivors of childhood abuse

This concept is included here as a reminder that people who grow up in violent families may be at high risk for domestic violence as adults.

Suggested Activities

1. In small groups, discuss the challenge of realistic goal formulation with clients and identify several strategies for balancing vision with reality. Develop and discuss an initial written contract related to those goals.

2.　　Arrange to visit a women's shelter in your community with the goal of obtaining a staff perspective of the experience of working there and learning more about the cycle of violence.

3. Invite a guest speaker to talk about the "Battered Woman's Movement" and where it is today, including what has been lost and gained along the way.

4. In small groups, develop a list of the most essential areas to explore at intake with Darlene, practice different ways of forming questions, and discuss the anxiety-producing aspects of working with this client along with ways to manage the anxiety.

References and Recommended Reading

Ell, K. (1996). Crisis theory and social work practice. In F. J. Turner (Ed.), *Social work treatment: Interlocking theoretical approaches.* (4th ed., pp. 296-340). New York: The Free Press.

Levy, B. (1995). Violence against women. In N. Van Den Bergh (Ed.), *Feminist practice in the 21st century* (pp. 312-329). Washington, DC: NASW Press.

Ogawa, B. (1996). *Walking on eggshells: Practical counseling for women in or leaving a violent relationship.* (3rd ed.). Volcano, CA: Volcano Press.

Stout, K. D., & McPhail, B. (1998). *Confronting sexism and violence against women: A challenge for social work.* New York: Longman.

Preserve the Family

The Agency

You are a worker for a special Family Preservation Unit that contracts with Child Protective Services (CPS). This agency specializes in intensive intervention with families in order to keep families together rather than removing children from their families and placing them in foster care. Workers have a limited caseload and are available to the families 24 hours a day for 90 days to offer support, resources, education, and crisis intervention services.

The Client System

Mrs. Jones (age 45) is an African-American mother of five who has been referred by CPS for your agency's intervention. Mrs. Jones is divorced from her fourth husband, and purportedly her last boyfriend had sex with her 14-year-old daughter, Nita, while Mrs. Jones was away. Nita is pregnant and has left home to live with an older sister. Mrs. Jones is now at home with a daughter (age 12), a son (age 16), and a stepson (age 10). Mrs. Jones has been unable to work due to the complications of diabetes.

When you interview Mrs. Jones, she appears remorseful over her daughter's leaving home and is angry at her boyfriend's behavior. She indicates that the boyfriend no longer comes around, although he has been in contact with her pregnant daughter. Nita has dropped out of school and is due to deliver in two months.

The other children are enrolled in school but are often absent. Mrs. Jones thinks that she has lost control of her children. The 16-year-old is showing signs of gang membership (staying out late, wearing colors). Mrs. Jones indicates that she wants to keep her family together.

Special Issues

Confidentiality is an issue that may be complicated by the intense nature of the preservation work with this family and the need to assess the safety of the children. This may set up some tension in the beginning of the working relationship. Other issues include health concerns that arise from the diagnosis of diabetes and teen pregnancy. Knowledge about the dynamics of gang membership and its attraction for teens in poverty is essential, as well as gathering information about gang prevention programs within the community. Family systems interventions and parenting skills will be important in this case.

Key Concepts and Principles

Family preservation
Planned efforts to provide the knowledge, resources, supports, health care, relationship skills and structures that help families stay intact and maintain their mutual roles and responsibilities (Barker, 1999).

Family system theory
Theory that emphasizes reciprocal relationships and mutual influence between individual family members and the whole and vice versa (Barker, 1999).

Suggested Activities

1. In small groups begin thinking about the case with respect to goals. Brainstorm three potential goals for work with the family. Analyze the goals to determine if they are measurable and achievable.

2. Divide the class into small groups. Each group develops a list of questions that they would want to ask to begin the assessment process in this case. Discuss each list.

3. Organize a panel of social workers from Planned Parenthood, CPS, a county health clinic, and a gang prevention program to discuss this case from each of their viewpoints. Topics might include possible interventions, resources available, and challenges. The case should be sent to the panel members ahead of time.

4. Show excerpts from the video, *Poverty Outlaw* about the Kensington Welfare Rights Union in which the union challenges some of the barriers to improved living conditions. Discuss the challenges of living in poverty, and how Mrs. Jones might be affected by membership in this support group.

5. Role play a family interview with all family members present. Two group members act as social workers. Assess the situation by asking each member to talk about their point of view regarding the problems facing their family. The group may be assigned to read the chapter on conducting an interview with a family in Lukas (1993).

6. Discuss the relationship between the boyfriend and Nita in light of sexual abuse issues, cultural understandings, and the roles of men and women within the African-American community.

7. View the videotape "Families in Crisis." This tape provides case scenarios of three family preservation programs emphasizing the role of the social worker. Discuss reactions to the tape and questions raised.

References and Recommended Reading

Barker, R. L. (1999). *The social work dictionary* (4th ed.). Washington, DC: NASW Press.

DeJong, P., & Miller, S. (1995). How to interview for client strengths. *Social Work, 40,* 729-736.

Devore, W., & Schlesinger, E. (1996). *Ethnic-sensitive social work practice* (4th ed.). Needham Heights, MA: Allyn and Bacon.

Hepworth, D., Rooney, R., & Larsen, J. A. (1997). *Direct social work practice: Theory and Skills* (5th ed.). Pacific Grove, CA: Brooks/Cole.

Kilpatrick, A. C., & Holland, T. P. (1995). *Working with families: An integrative model by level of functioning.* Needham Heights, MA: Allyn and Bacon.

Lukas, S. (1993). *Where to start and what to ask: An assessment handbook,* New York: Norton.

Moyers, B. (1991). Families in Crisis. In Edna McConnell Clark Foundation (Producer), *Families First with Bill Moyers.* New York and Washington, DC: Public Broadcasting Service.

Yates, P. (Producer/Director), & Kinoy, P. (Producer/Director). 1997. *Poverty Outlaw.* [Video]. (Available from Skylight Pictures, Inc., 330 W. 42nd Street, New York, NY 10036).

Unit II

The Middle Phase: Energizing the Work

Chapter 7

Intervention Planning

An intervention in a professional relationship is any verbal or behavioral act, the purpose of which is to influence the process or outcome of the interaction in order to achieve mutual goals. Intervention planning implies actions that are carefully considered and purposeful, and are based on professional, individualized assessment and partnership with the client.

Recovery: A Nonlinear Process

The Agency

The agency in this case is actually one program in a large public "umbrella" agency that is funded by state, county, and city monies. In a metropolitan area with a population of three-quarters of a million people, this is the only inpatient facility for indigent, chemically dependent clients, and there are only 30 beds. The program has a long waiting list and is struggling to keep its doors open in the face of continuing funding cuts. Most of the clients served are male.

The Client System

Mr. Hernan (age 47) is a white male who has been in inpatient treatment at a public, nonprofit facility for chemical dependency for two weeks of a four-week treatment program. He has been involved in all aspects of the treatment, which is based on a 12-step program and includes two individual sessions with the social worker each week. When he entered treatment on a court order as a condition for probation, you were assigned to work with him and have now seen him a total of four times.

Mr. Hernan is divorced with five children. He has been addicted to heroin for years, with a history of periods of staying clean before relapse. He has expressed a great deal of pain regarding feeling unloved and unwanted in his family of origin and believes that he has worked unsuccessfully all of his life to be loved and recognized. He would very much like to be reunited with his ex-wife. Mr. Hernan grew up in a large city and has a tenth grade education. He has worked a number of blue-collar jobs including driving a cab. He has never done jail time and denies ever selling drugs.

Although not formally religious, Mr. Hernan does have an active spiritual life, and has impressed staff with his ability to express feelings at a deep level. He has also done very well in addressing issues in his recovery. This includes taking responsibility for his addiction rather than finding external factors to blame for his using.

Special Issues

Special issues to consider in working with this case include the difficulty of reconciling confrontation and self-determination in working with chemical dependency, the practice difficulties in dealing with dually diagnosed clients, and the question of whether workers who are not in recovery themselves can work effectively with people who are drug/alcohol addicted. Another important issue for social workers in the chemical dependency field is how to individualize clients within a 12-Step treatment format.

In planning how to work with Mr. Hernan, it is important to consider the ways in which he may be at risk for relapse since recovery, like human growth, is not a linear process. Many addicts relapse several times before attaining lasting sobriety.

Key Concepts and Principles

Behavior is purposeful
> People do not continue in behavior patterns unless those behaviors serve some need. What may be a problem in the present was probably adaptive in the past.

Client empowerment
> A concept closely related to self-determina-

tion, based on the premise that the more choices clients recognize they have, the more proactive they can be in their own lives by claiming their power to choose.

Relapse in recovery

Since addiction is generally considered a chronic disease, it is common for addicts to relapse several times before attaining lasting sobriety. Any recovering addict or alcoholic may be in danger of relapse even with years of being drug/alcohol free.

Suggested Activities

1. Identify ten key exploratory questions for the worker to assess intervention options with Mr. Hernan. Discuss your rationale and explain why you identified them as important.

2. List external factors that would need to be present to support Mr. Hernan's continued sobriety and prepare him for the dangers of relapse. What are the policy/program implications for the agency?

3. Become familiar with the 12-Step program, or read part of the "Big Book" (the guide for recovering alcoholics, available at open AA meeetings). Share your individual impressions, and make at least one suggestion to make the 12-Step program more sensitive to women and ethnic minorities.

4. Attend an open 12-Step meeting and prepare reflective notes to share in class. Include both positive impressions and areas of discomfort.

References and Recommended Reading

Addiction Technology Transfer Centers, National Curriculum Committee (1998). *Addiction counseling competencies: The knowledge, skills, and professional attitudes of professional practice.* Rockville, MD: US Department of Health and Human Resources.

Gorski, T. T. (1989). *Understanding the twelve steps.* Independence, MO: Herald House/Independence Press.

Straussner, S. (Ed.). (1993). *Clinical work with substance abusing clients.* New York: Guilford.

Speaking Out

The Agency

You are a caseworker on staff at a state Adult Protective Services agency. The agency's mandate is to investigate allegations of abuse, neglect, or exploitation of dependent adults over the age of 65 and persons with disabilities. You, along with the other workers, have ongoing individual caseloads of approximately 75 clients each. In addition to the initial investigation on each case, you are responsible for extensive documentation, maintenance of the case file (including interventions), and follow-up on any subsequent information regarding the clients assigned to your caseload.

The Client System

Sam (age 30) is a white male who lives in a rural area with Mary, his caregiver, who is paid through the Medicaid program to provide care to Sam who is quadriplegic, homebound, incontinent, and requires assistance with all activities of daily living, including bathing, dressing, and eating. The Medicaid program provides a nurse to oversee Sam's medical care. Approximately a year ago a complaint was filed with Adult Protective Services by a Meals on Wheels volunteer who reported hearing "Mary shouting and cussing at Sam." Another time she said she heard Mary say to Sam, "I'll make you pay, you crippled bastard. I'm sick of taking care of you," followed by slapping sounds. When the volunteer entered the room, Sam was bleeding from the corner of his mouth and she saw Mary kick a metal studded leather strap on the floor under the bed. At the time of the report you, the caseworker, did a complete investigation. Although there was evidence of abuse, Sam denied any wrongdoing on the part of Mary and did not want protective services. Since he had the right to refuse services, you filed the appropriate documentation, took no action, but kept the file open.

Your supervisor has forwarded a phone call to you. It is Sam, who with the aid of the nurse assigned to his care, has called Adult Protective Services to ask for assistance in being removed from Mary's care. He says to you, "Please get Mary out of here. She's crazy, and I'm afraid when she comes back, she is going to kill me." He goes on to say that Mary has left him alone to visit her sister until the next day. You arrange to make a home visit within the hour. The nurse indicates she will stay with Sam until you arrive.

Special Issues

While Child Protective Services cannot be refused, adults can refuse intervention by Adult Protective Services and cannot be removed from their residence without their consent unless they are adjudicated incompetent. Since a perpetrator may use intimidation, coercion, or threats toward a victim, it is sometimes difficult to determine if a victim has the capacity or opportunity to ask for assistance.

Another issue concerns the caseload that workers carry in protective services. Usually there is little time to do a thorough investigation except with cases designated "Priority One" (imminent risk of physical harm).

Key Concepts and Principles

Adult Protective Services

Services furnished to an elderly or disabled person who has been determined to be in a state of abuse, neglect, or exploitation. These services may include social casework, case management, and arranging psychiatric and health evaluation, home care, social services, and health care (Barker, 1999).

Client competency

The capacity to understand and act upon the understanding. A client may be competent in one area of life and incompetent in others.

Elder abuse

The negligent or willful infliction of injury, unreasonable confinement, intimidation, or cruel punishment with resulting physical or emotional harm or pain by a caretaker, family member, or other individual with whom the elderly or disabled person has an ongoing relationship.

Suggested Activities

1. Role play the interview between Sam and the social worker in order to determine the client's competency and plan for next steps.

2. Review the state regulations for Adult Protective Services and Child Protective Services and discuss the difference between the two.

3. Examine the differences among adult abuse, neglect, and exploitation.

4. Investigate the standards by which an adult is adjudicated incompetent.

5. Review your state's Adult Protective Services code of ethics. Determine which sections apply to this case.

References and Recommended Reading

Barker, R. L. (1999). *The social work dictionary* (4th ed.). Washington, DC: NASW Press.

DuBois, B., & Miley, K. K. (1996). *Social work: An empowering profession*. Needham Heights, MA: Allyn and Bacon.

Johnson, H. W. (1998). *The social services: An introduction* (5th ed.). Itasca, IL: F. E. Peacock.

Loewenberg, F. M., & Dolgoff, R. (1996). *Ethical decisions for social work practice* (5th ed.). Itasca, IL: F. E. Peacock.

Sporting Chance—Part II

(Refer to Sporting Chance—Part I in Chapter 5)

The Agency

You are a social worker within a visiting teacher program in a local school district, which includes approximately 60,000 students. Populations served are white, African-American, Hispanic, Asian, Native American, and refugees from Cuba, Central and South America, and the former Yugoslavia. The visiting teacher program includes personnel with professional experience as teachers, social workers, and counselors. Most of the work is referred by teachers and counselors, but any school employee can refer students whose behavior gives the appearance of personal or social problems. The visiting teacher gathers pertinent data regarding the situation from school personnel, the student, and the family system to ascertain problem areas and develop plans for intervention. School-based resources include school psychologists, special education specialists, and teachers, as well as various community-based services for children and youth. Most of the work involves group services, individual and family counseling, program development and consultation for classroom teachers and school counselors.

The Client System

Victor (age 15), a Hispanic male, and several other baseball and track team members whose participation in team sports is in jeopardy due to poor grades have agreed to meet with the social worker to facilitate their return to full participation in sports. Group members must attend these meetings during the early morning "advisory period," requiring their arrival to school in a more timely manner. The coaches and respective parents have given written approval.

Victor had been seen associating with students who are known to be gang members and users of various drugs. Also, during the last six-week period, his grades dipped into low B and C levels, a distinct shift from his previous A and B performance. He also missed classes and baseball practice. Kenny (age 15), a white male, attends school regularly but is having major problems in Algebra I. He also has an "attitude problem," according to the track coach. Robert (age 15), a Hispanic male, plays baseball. He is extremely talented but resents being on the freshman team. His father, a former high school baseball star, agrees that Robert should be in the varsity team, and he has been to the school to give the coach "pointers on how to challenge the players" to do their very best. Malcolm (age 15), an African-American male, looks much older than the other boys and is also a talented player. He holds a part-time job four hours each night and on weekends. His goal is to buy a car by the end of the school year. He attends school regularly but often falls asleep during classes. Jorge (age 15), a Hispanic male from South America, attends school regularly and plays baseball well but is so shy that his team work and his class performance suffer. The baseball coach wonders if Jorge can take the peer pressure. Frequently, Jorge seems to find reasons to leave practice early. Finally, Bryan (age 15), a white male, is on the track team. His grades are failing, and he is late arriving to school several times a week.

You have approval to offer a six-week group program focusing on personal goal setting and orientation for success in high school. Another social worker, a male who was once successful in sports, may join you as a co-leader.

Special Issues

Although the group members agreed to meet as a group, their primary motivation appears to be their return to full participation in sports. Thus the group is quasi-involuntary, which presents some group work issues. Also, the group is comprised of ethnically diverse members, requiring multicultural awareness and skills on the part of the social worker, as well as knowledge about intervention planning with groups.

Key Concepts and Principles

Group stages

Groups are identified by various stages of growth including group formation, initial trust-building, transition, working, and ending (Corey & Corey, 1997).

Intervention planning with groups

Individual and group sessions concerning the purpose, rules, goals, and process of the group as well as the goals of the individual members.

Suggested Activities

1. Conduct the "Multicultural Awareness Knowledge, and Skills Survey." (Corey & Corey, 1997).

2. Reflect on your knowledge about high schools and athletic programs. Then, list characteristics of a high school that is competent in relating to the cultural and economic differences of its constituencies.

3. Role play the third session with this group, paying particular attention to progress on personal goal setting.

4. Discuss the impact of the group leader in terms of gender, ethnicity, and familiarity with sports.

References and Recommended Reading

Corey, M. S., & Corey, G. (1997). *Groups: Process and practice* (5th ed.). Pacific Grove, CA: Brooks/Cole.

Sue, D. W., Carter, R.T., Casas, J. M., Fouad, N. A., Ivey, A. E., Jensen, M., LaFromboise, T., Manese, J. E., Ponterotto, J. G., & Vasquez-Nutall, E. (1998). *Multicultural counseling competencies: Individual and organizational development.* Thousand Oaks, CA: Sage.

Chapter 8

Ongoing Assessment

Ongoing assessment can be
conceptualized as a product, such as
a written evaluation or document.
It is also a continuous process
from the first hello through the last
good-bye. From that perspective,
our thinking about clients does
not become rigid or fixed but is
constantly changing with new
information.

Finding Her Voice

The Agency

The Learning Center is a non-profit agency that provides educational and job training services to youth and young adults who have dropped out of public school. Participants must meet eligibility requirements based on income at or below the poverty line. African-American and Hispanic students make up the majority of the student body, with whites and Asian-Americans constituting the minority. Counselors at the agency and some of the supervisor/trainers are social workers. Social workers provide support, case management, crisis intervention, and ongoing counseling as needed to help insure the participants' success in the program. Individual services are provided, especially initially, based on what has been aptly dubbed "the hanging out model"—the informal, low-key, respectful approach the staff utilizes to establish rapport and trust with the participants.

The Client System

Amy (age 16) is a white female referred by her previous high school counselor. A social worker met Amy several months ago and began working with her individually and in two groups. The groups included one co-ed, all-classroom, open support group and an all-female closed support group, "Celebrate Me," which was also psychoeducational. "Celebrate Me" was designed to foster positive self-image related to feminist issues as they applied to adolescent girls. In addition to these formal contacts, in keeping with the agency culture and mission, there have been many informal contacts throughout the school year. It was not until later, after the relationship with Amy was firmly established, that Amy confided to the worker that she struggled with a problem with food that included bingeing and purging. This revelation was a huge step for Amy since she felt so much shame about this problem.

Amy lives with her mother, a sister (age 18), a nephew (age 2), and a niece (age 1), in low income, Section 8 housing. The family receives Temporary Assistance for Needy Families, Medicaid, and food stamps. Amy is very close to her mother, but has no contact with her father. Both of Amy's older sisters became pregnant when they were 16, and both have two children each. At one time, Amy was under medical treatment for the bulimia, although Amy claims that she has not binged or purged for three months. Amy's concern is that she has no one to talk with about the problem and that if she gains more weight or does not do well in school, she will not be able to resist the impulse to binge and purge. She does not want to upset her mother, and no one else in the family knows about the eating disorder. At this time, she is not ready to disclose to her group.

Special Issues

Given the mandate of the agency, one obvious issue in this case is to clarify what a social worker can and cannot do to help Amy with her eating disorder. As is frequently the case with clients, Amy may need to talk with someone about her concerns, but is not necessarily ready to take any action on her own behalf.

Many young people who suffer from eating disorders are often very ashamed and reluctant to let anyone know their secret. The fact that Amy is unwilling to share her issues with the group may mean that she is in greater danger of relapse. Yet, if the worker is overzealous in attempting to get Amy to open up in group, Amy could withdraw or drop out all together.

Key Concepts and Principles

Nonlinear problem-solving process
> While the problem-solving process is conceptualized in stages (data collection, assessment, intervention, evaluation), in practice those stages overlap and intertwine with constant shifting from one to another.

Exploration
> This process involves much more than just obtaining facts. It includes probing under the surface and into the meaning of the client experiences.

Suggested Activities

1. Identify some of the key considerations in ongoing assessment in this case. What will the worker need to monitor and what might be the basis for deciding whether to involve the family?

2. Discuss Bulimia Nervosa and include students' previous reading and knowledge about the subject. Invite students to share any professional experience or curiosity about the topic. Brainstorm possible ways to help Amy.

3. In a small group exercise, plan a group session designed to encourage discussion of the topic in a safe, nonjudgmental climate.

4. Research the prevalence of eating disorders by ethnic groups and the implications for both micro and macro interventions and report findings at the next class.

5. Make a list of Amy's individual, relationship, and community strengths. Note obstacles and aspects of her life that may interfere with her continued recovery. What are the implications for the worker? For the community?

References and Recommended Reading

Gutierrez, L. (1991). Empowering women of color: A feminist model. In M. Bricker-Jenkins, N. Hooyman, & N. Gottlieg (Eds.), *Feminist social work practice in clinical settings* (pp. 199-214). Newbury Park: Sage.

Hepworth, D. H., Rooney, R. H., & Larsen, J. A. (1997). *Direct social work practice: Theory and skills* (5th ed.). Pacific Grove, CA: Brooks/Cole.

Loewenberg, F. M., & Dolgoff, R. (1996). *Ethical decisions for social work practice* (5th ed.). Itasca, IL: F. E. Peacock.

Pipher, M. B. (1994). *Reviving Ophelia: Saving the selves of adolescent girls.* New York: Ballantine.

So Many Mountains to Climb

The Agency

The agency is a nonprofit organization whose mission is to serve women who have been sexually assaulted or molested. Although rape crisis services are an inherent part of the agency's program, community education and therapy services, both individual and group, are offered for women who have been sexually abused as children. Since this is one of a very few places offering sliding scale fees or pro bono counseling to those who are unable to pay anything, the demand for longer term counseling for survivors of sexual abuse has created a lengthy waiting list. The agency has experienced tremendous growing pains in the last five years as it has struggled to keep pace with the demand for services without sacrificing quality. The agency maintains close ties with local law enforcement authorities and public mental health agencies.

The Client System

Linda (age 31) is a white, married mother of three sons. She identifies herself as a Jehovah's Witness although she was not raised in this tradition. Linda first came to the agency seeking help a few months ago when she began experiencing memories of childhood sexual abuse. After an extensive intake interview, you have seen her weekly for eight weeks with another four months remaining to work with her.

Linda described her family of origin as "appearing perfect." There was no known mental illness or chemical abuse. Her mother did not work outside the home, and her father was a white-collar professional. Linda is not particularly close to any of her family, although she is aware that one sister is currently in therapy.

Linda has two years of college and has worked part time as an administrative assistant in a state agency since her youngest child reached the age of two. Her husband is an engineer whom she describes as very supportive of her. Their sons are ages eight, five, and three.

Linda began having what she describes as "flashbacks" (i.e., memories so vivid that she felt like the remembered events were happening in the present and that she was in them). The first of these occurred after a visit from her parents a few months prior to her coming into the agency. She finds it particularly distressing that she cannot remember who the perpetrator was, but believes it was her uncle or father or both. The flashbacks have decreased, but she continues to feel "numb," and says that she would like to remember everything without the painful feelings. Linda often feels "out of control," "terrible" about herself, and has very little self-confidence. She would like to be able to feel her feelings without losing control.

Special Issues

The title of this case is appropriate because of the complexity of the issues with adult survivors of childhood sexual abuse. It is important not to assume, however, that every survivor was severely traumatized and later incapacitated in adulthood.

One concern is how the worker can be helpful to this client while being mindful of the potential for setting up the client and the worker for accusations of generating painful but inaccurate memories. This is not only a clinical issue but an agency policy issue as well. Good interviewing skills are crucial.

Another issue is how to contract with this client around realistic goals. The worker must consider how the old trauma is affecting Linda's daily life now. The client must have enough ego strength and daily stability to justify any attempt to delve more deeply into her painful past. Helping her manage her symptoms and discussing the possibility of a referral for an evaluation for medical intervention should she become overwhelmed and unable to execute her daily responsibilities, are key factors here.

Key Concepts and Principles

Repressed or false memory in clients
> Therapists are at risk for accusations that "false" memories of abuse occurred as a result of the therapeutic process rather than recovering "true" but repressed memories.

Suggested Activities

1. In small groups, suggest a tentative diagnosis for Linda and identify some of the implications of that diagnosis for treatment.

2. In two separate groups develop an argument on both sides of the false memory debate.

Present the arguments in class. What safeguards can be suggested to protect workers and clients from charges of raising false allegations of child abuse?

3. Discuss clients who believe they are victims of satanic abuse, or other "incredible" experiences. What should the worker consider in listening to the stories and working with these clients? What about clients whom you believe to be fabricating or lying about their experiences?

4. Role play interviewing skills that do not "lead the witness" or "plant ideas" in the client's mind.

References and Recommended Reading

Compton, B. R., & Galaway, B. (1999). *Social work processes* (6th ed.). Pacific Grove: Brooks/Cole.

Daley, D. C., & Thase, M. E. (1994). *Dual disorders recovery counseling*. Independence, MO: Herald House.

Evans, K., & Sullivan, J. M. (1995). *Treating addicted survivors of trauma*. New York: Guilford.

Loftus, E., & Ketcham, K. (1994). *The myth of repressed memory: False memories and allegations of sexual abuse*. New York: St. Martin's.

Chapter 9

Implementation

Implementation is the phase of the client/worker relationship characterized by the client carrying out the plan of intervention.

New Beginnings—Part II

(Refer to New Beginnings—Part I in Chapter 3)

The Agency

New Beginnings is a community mental health clinic with 50 staff members offering individual, family, couples, and group treatment for children, adolescents, and adults. The agency has a sliding fee scale. Agency workers come from a variety of professional backgrounds and are prepared to assist clients experiencing depression, anxiety disorders, posttraumatic stress disorder, and other mental health concerns. You are one of several social workers providing treatment.

The Client System

Margaret Hernandez (age 38), an attractive Hispanic homemaker, is seeking services from New Beginnings. Margaret tells you that about a year ago, during an early evening jog at a local running and biking trail, she was raped by a male acquaintance from her gym. Margaret has been in counseling for two months at New Beginnings. Weekly, Margaret attends both a women's support group and individual counseling. The group is specifically for women, 18 and over, who are survivors of sexual assault. Margaret has shared her feelings of rage and shame, as well as learned that her reactions to the assault are normal; in fact, she found that all of the women in the group reacted as she had to their own assaults. The group has helped Margaret to feel more normal and accepted, and less "guilty" about the assault.

Margaret also meets with you, the social worker for one hour each week, to discuss her concern over the depression and anxiety brought on by the assault. Margaret has made slow, but steady progress. During the first two meetings, you gathered information about Margaret's assault, her family, and her panic attacks. After these meetings, you and Margaret formulated two initial goals to work on. The first goal was for Margaret to manage her anxiety. In order to achieve this goal, cognitive-behavioral techniques were employed to help Margaret change her thoughts and behaviors when she felt panic or strong emotion erupting. To create a new behavioral response, you helped Margaret to learn relaxation techniques and ways to channel feelings, such as journal writing and calling friends.

Margaret's second goal was to regain control of her home life, although you both agreed that this was a long-term goal that must be broken into small, manageable steps. Margaret's first task was to develop a list of everything that needed to be done in her house. Next, she decided upon priority items, and who in her family was capable of performing these tasks. Currently, you and Margaret are working on a plan that she can present to her family when they all meet for a family session in the near future. At this point, Margaret has been able to share some of her frustration about having all the household responsibilities for her family.

Special Issues

The idea of returning a sense of personal control to victims of any traumatic experience is a key part of healing, and thus, a key part of crisis intervention. The trauma, in this case a sexual assault, took away Margaret's belief that the world is a safe place for her. Although Margaret presents many concerns that are worthy of examination, it is crucial to her emotional and physical well-being that she learn once again that she has some control over life.

Key Concepts and Principles

Resilience

Having the strengths, social skills, and personal characteristics to help an individual resist or rebound from difficult experiences.

Crisis intervention

The therapeutic practice used in helping clients in crisis to promote effective coping that can lead to positive growth and change. This is achieved through acknowledging the problem, recognizing its impact, and learning new or more effective behaviors of coping with similar predictable experiences. (Barker, 1999).

Task-centered treatment

A system of brief, time-limited practice that emphasizes helping clients with specific problems of their own choosing through discrete client and practitioner actions or tasks (Reid, 1996).

Suggested Activities

1. Role play a family meeting where Margaret shares her frustration about handling most of the household responsibilities. Set up two or three tasks on which the family would work.

2. Discuss and practice three cognitive-behav-ioral techniques that could help Margaret manage anxiety.

3. Invite a social worker to class to speak about posttraumatic stress.

4. Invite a representative from the criminal justice system to talk with the class about the legal rights of sexual assault victims.

References and Recommended Reading

Barker, R. L. (1999). *The social work dictionary* (4th ed.). Washington, DC: NASW Press.

Ell, K. (1996). Crisis theory and social work practice. In F. J. Turner (Ed.), *Social work treatment: Interlocking theoretical approaches* (pp. 168-190). New York: The Free Press.

Herman, J. (1997). *Trauma and recovery: The aftermath of violence—from domestic abuse to political terror.* New York: Basic Books.

Thomlinson, B., & Thomlinson, R. J. (1996). Behavior theory and social work treatment. In F. J. Turner (Ed.), *Social work treatment: Interlocking theoretical approaches* (pp. 39-68). New York: The Free Press.

Ledray, L. E. (1994). *Recovering from rape.* New York: Henry Holt and Co.

Lukas, S. (1993). How to conduct the first interview with a child. *Where to start and what to ask: An assessment handbook* (pp. 58-77). New York: Norton.

Matsakis, A. (1994). *Post-traumatic stress disorder: A complete treatment guide.* Oakland, CA: New Harbinger.

Reid, W. (1996). Task centered social work practice. In F. J. Turner (Ed.), *Social work treatment: Interlocking theoretical approaches* (pp. 617-640). New York: The Free Press.

Lantz, J. (1996). Cognitive theory and social work treatment. In F. J. Turner (Ed.), *Social work treatment: Interlocking theoretical approaches* (pp. 94-115). New York: The Free Press.

A Child No More

The Agency

You are a school-based social worker in a system that has decentralized services throughout an urban school district. You are not employed by the district; therefore, you must work with school personnel to identify potential service recipients. In the event that a student seeks services independently, you must clear the self-referral with the school counselor. Above all else, you must follow school policies. One such policy requires that you communicate all health-related information to parents as quickly as possible. Your employing agency, however, emphasizes confidentiality for clients.

The Client System

Miriam (age 16), a white high school junior, is fidgety and obviously anxious when she arrives at the social work office. In your initial contact, Miriam focuses on how she has been unable to concentrate on her school work, and how her grades are rapidly falling. In fact, her work has gone from high B's and low A's to C's and possibly a failing grade this semester. In later sessions, Miriam tells you that her boyfriend (age 17) "dumped her" for another girl, then suddenly started dating her again, and now is asking her to "give him space." During the last three months they have been sexually active with no protection. Miriam has skipped one menstrual period and believes she has a mild case of morning sickness. She has not shared this concern with anyone else and is most fearful of sharing it with her mother, a single parent, who apparently sacrificed much to help one child graduate from high school and get Miriam this far. Miriam's father sends some money on a monthly basis but is otherwise uninvolved.

Miriam is overweight and appears older than her years. She has blunted affect, speaks in a low voice and keeps her eyes on her hands. She has some of the brand name items worn by other students, but in general she is not dressed like most of the others her age. Miriam has no history of "trouble-making" and is frequently on the honor role.

Miriam's perfect attendance in the past has been replaced with consistent tardiness and absenteeism. School policy dictates that she cannot be promoted if she has any further absences.

Special Issues

Teen pregnancy, school-based social work limitations, and teen parenting need to be considered.

Key Concepts and Principles

Confidentiality

The protection of clients' private information, revealed during the helping process, is essential to the development of a collaborative relationship between the client and the professional social worker (Hepworth, Rooney, & Larsen, 1997). There are, however, limits on confidentiality when shared information portends actual or potential harm to the client, others, or both.

Teen pregnancy

When an adolescent girl becomes pregnant, there may be concerns due to health, education, and economic implications, as well as the psychosocial and emotional impact. The young girl, the father of the baby, and both of their families may feel these effects.

School social work

School social work, also known as school-based social work, refers to the provision of social work services within an educational setting, most often in a public school system.

Suggested Activities

1. Discuss value differences and ethical issues involved in providing services to Miriam, paying particular attention to the ethical issues inherent in working as a social worker in a host setting.

2. Role play the first contact with Miriam as a member of a different cultural group. Discuss similarities and differences in your approach.

3. Borrow a "virtual baby" and ask a member of the class to care for the baby one weekend and log the activity involved in providing adequate care for this child. ("Virtual babies" are electronic games designed to communicate the needs of an infant.)

4. Invite a panel of teenage parents, both mothers and fathers, to present their perspectives on their experiences.

5. Visit a local maternity home or a school-based program for teenagers with children. What issues/needs do teenage parents (both genders) face with an unwanted or unexpected pregnancy? What policy changes has the school made to address the special needs of the young mothers and their children? What staffing and staff training changes were necessary?

6. Invite a culturally diverse panel of parents of teenagers with children. What can they tell the class about how the pregnancy has influenced their families? What are the value differences? Are there cultural differences?

References and Recommended Reading

Hepworth, D. H., Rooney, R. H., & Larsen, J. A. (1997). *Direct social work practice: Theory and skills* (5th ed.). Pacific Grove, CA: Brooks/Cole.

Lowenberg, R. D., & Dolgoff, R. (1996). *Ethical decisions for social work practice* (5th ed.). Itasca, IL: F. E. Peacock.

Chapter 10

Planning for Evaluation

Planning for evaluation is the social work skill of forming a procedure or method for assessing the effectiveness of an intervention strategy.

Homebound

The Agency

You are a social worker at Total Health, Inc., a privately owned, for-profit home health agency with offices throughout the United States. You receive referrals from the coordinator at the agency. Total Health, Inc. serves a diverse group of clients from all income levels and is funded primarily through Medicare reimbursement, although insurance company reimbursement provides for the care of adults and children under the age of 65.

The Client System

Mrs. Boyton (age 58) is an African-American widow who moved to the area approximately six months ago following a brief hospitalization due to a hip fracture. She lives in the back room of her daughter's home. You have been visiting the client regularly and have gathered the following information. Mrs. Boyton sold her home and now pays her daughter $40.00 a month for the use of the back room. She has a sister who lives in the area and two other daughters, both of whom live out-of-state. Mrs. Boyton's daughter and husband appear to be a hard working, African-American couple who have both worked for years to establish themselves in a "nice neighborhood." After raising a son and daughter, they continue to hold several jobs in order to pay off a mortgage, their automobiles, and a recreational vehicle that they use to go on fishing trips. The daughter is primarily employed as a cook in a school cafeteria; the son-in-law is a supervisor in a local industrial plant.

Mrs. Boyton received rehabilitation from the home health physical therapist and was able to transfer independently from wheelchair to toilet and wheelchair to bed. At the time of her discharge from medical services, it appeared that the client's improved physical status, combined with her daughter's willingness to provide care, would result in a positive situation for the client. However, in the last three weeks she has stayed in a wheelchair during the day, says she "cannot control things," and that she is too slow and weak to make it to the toilet on time. Consequently, when the daughter returns home from work, she spends some time each day cleaning her mother and the wheelchair. Furthermore, Mrs. Boyton sometimes goes without breakfast and lunch and has little appetite for dinner. As a result she has lost 30 pounds in the last seven months and looks frail and increasingly disheveled. The daughter declares, "I can't possibly cook her breakfast and lunch…I have to get to work," and she goes on to say "Ever since my mother moved in, all my husband and I do is argue." Mrs. Boyton tells you she is sleeping less and less and that she is concerned about her failing memory and her incontinence. She wonders if these are signs of impending death. Above all, she hopes to die without going to a nursing home. When asked about her care, Mrs. Boyton, responds. "My daughter is a good daughter and takes care of me."

Special Issues

Caring for aging parents is a significant and sometimes unexpected role for adult children. They are often unprepared for the stress involved in caring for a parent and receive little support for their efforts. As far as the aging parent is concerned, a number of losses are sustained prior to making the move into the adult child's home and depression is a frequent result.

Key Concepts and Principles

Caregiver burden

The accumulated stress felt by an individual who provides for the emotional, physical, and social needs of another person.

Depression in older adults

Depressive symptoms which differ from those of younger adults may include disorientation, forgetfulness, angry outbursts, and lowered functioning in activities of daily living (in addition to other symptoms of depression).

Value orientation

The characteristic way individuals or groups look at their own and others' standards of conduct, moral principles, and social customs.

Suggested Activities

1. The social worker has arranged a meeting with the client and the client's daughter and son-in-law. Role play the meeting with attention to evaluating the present situation.

2. From the references listed at the end of this case, research the signs and symptoms of late life depression and indicate their applicability to this case.

3. Discuss the relevance of age, ethnicity, economic status, and gender in this situation.

4. List resources that may be available to this client system.

5. Explore social policy issues involved in this client situation. What are the unmet needs in your community? In your state? In this country?

References and Recommended Reading

Aiken, L. R. (1998). *Human development in adulthood*. New York: Plenum.

Burlingame, V. S. (1999). *Ethnogerocounseling: Counseling ethnic elders and their families*. New York: Springer.

Butler, R. N., Lewis, M. I., & Sunderland, T. (1998). *Aging and mental health: Positive psychosocial and biomedical approaches* (5th ed.). Needham Heights, MA: Allyn and Bacon.

Family Hopes

The Agency

As a social worker serving on an interdisciplinary team within a small, nonprofit agency whose target client population is children with developmental disorders (newborn through age 5) and their families, you are responsible for providing support services within the home setting. This agency serves children who are referred by school districts, government agencies, and health care providers for both assessment and therapeutic interventions. Social work interventions include assessment and case management, supportive parent and family counseling, skill training and role modeling of cognitive and behavioral strategies, stress management and respite services, and support groups for parents and siblings.

The Client System

Alexis (age 3) is a white female with Down's Syndrome who has been referred by her pediatrician for services. You have been working with her and her family for about six months and have successfully developed a comprehensive assessment and treatment plan. In addition to professional social work services, Alexis is receiving both occupational therapy and speech therapy through this agency.

Alexis is the youngest of three children born to Don (age 46) and Nancy (age 42). The two older siblings—boys, ages seven and nine—are both developing age appropriately. Alexis was a planned for and very much desired child. Shortly after Alexis' birth, Nancy developed symptoms of acute depression and refused to care for the infant. At that time, Nancy's mother was staying with the family and providing daily support. Both the maternal grandmother and Don encouraged Nancy to seek a consultation with a physician for what seemed to be an unusually severe postpartum reaction to the grief and loss issues associated with the Down's diagnosis.

Nancy was given a referral by her obstetrician for counseling and has been seeing a psychiatrist weekly for about five months. She has also been taking prescribed antidepressants for that time period as well, and has reported a marked improvement in her mood and acceptance of Alexis. The grandmother continues to remain in the home, with Nancy gradually resuming some of the daily care for the baby.

As the social worker, your assessment included identification of needs, goals and intervention strategies. You have been providing services through home visits, phone consults, and bi-weekly office sessions with members of the family. The youngest son has been referred recently for a special education assessment to determine if a learning disability exists. He reportedly is reading two levels below grade level. The older son's classroom teacher has contacted the parents with concerns about an increase in "acting out behaviors and anger management issues."

Special Issues

Sensitivity to the issues of grief and loss surrounding the birth of this child have guided the development of an intervention plan for this family. However, ancillary issues within the family context still need to be addressed. It is also important to establish a collaborative interdisciplinary relationship with the psychiatrist as well as the other members of the agency's team who are providing service.

Key Concepts and Principles

Client advocacy

> To secure services that the client needs and is entitled to but is unable to obtain on his or her own (Sheafor, 1997).

Personal empowerment

> The process of helping individuals to increase their personal, interpersonal, socioeconomic, and political strength and to develop influence toward improving their circumstances (Barker, 1999).

Suggested Activities

1. Evaluate the progress made by the client and assess the areas of work. What is the plan to evaluate the efficacy of interventions?

2. Brainstorm in small class groups a list for each family member of needs, goals, and intervention strategies that would be in place during this middle phase of the helping process.

3. Develop activities that would support the intervention strategies. Students individually and in small groups present in-class demonstrations of implementation (i.e., through role plays, video clips, guest speakers etc.).

4. Research community resources for this family.

5. Conduct an in-class facilitated discussion around the issue of unexpected loss. Have students write a five minute reflection on that topic.

References and Recommended Reading

Barker, R. L. (1999). *The social work dictionary* (4th ed.). Washington, DC: NASW Press.

Kushner, H. S. (1981). *When bad things happen to good people.* New York: Schocken Books.

Sheafor, B. W., Horejsi, C. R., & Horejsi, G. A. (1997). *Techniques and guidelines for social work practice* (4th ed.). Needham Heights, MA: Allyn and Bacon

Small, J. (1990). *Becoming naturally therapeutic—A return to the true essence of helping.* New York: Bantam.

Chapter 11

Overcoming Obstacles to Change

To formulate realistic goals with clients, one must mutually identify and examine relationship and environmental/situational factors that could preclude or inhibit success.

A Path to Renewal

The Agency

Howell House is a residential treatment center for women who are addicted to any chemical substance. It is one of a very few centers to allow women to bring their children, and in which children are also treated. It is a nonprofit, private agency that is funded through the state alcohol and drug commission, fundraisers, grants, and United Way. Staff includes a clinical director who is a social worker, another staff social worker, an executive director with a degree in business, several licensed chemical dependency counselors, and a nurse. Morale in this agency is generally high because staff are invited to participate in creating new and innovative programs for the residents. In addition to the intense residential treatment component, there is a halfway house for the women to live in when they are able and stable enough to find employment. The average length of stay in the first program is 18 months; in the halfway house, it is three to six months.

The Client System

Monica (age 33) is a white female. Currently she is an unemployed college student, existing on federal aid while she pursues a career in electronics. The father of Monica's eight-year-old son, to whom Monica has been married for nine years, is currently in prison for selling narcotics. Although legally she is still married, and she still communicates with her husband through letters, Monica considers herself divorced. She has several good female friends, and, after 20 years of substance abuse, she is active in Alcohol Anonymous and has four years of sobriety. Monica was in residential treatment for about a year and a half in Howell House. Since then she has participated in an aftercare group which meets once a week.

The director of the aftercare program referred Monica to you when Monica expressed a desire to have individual therapy in lieu of group work. You have been seeing Monica once a week for approximately six months.

Monica was raised in a working-class family, with two alcoholic parents who were frequently violent when they were drunk. Monica's paternal grandmother took care of her most of the time, and when she was with this grandmother she felt protected and "spoiled." By the age of 16, Monica was drinking and smoking marijuana on a regular basis. She was raped at age 19, and began using heroin shortly thereafter. Monica has difficulty maintaining healthy boundaries and is socially immature, which makes her at high risk for selecting companions who will abuse her.

Monica came to see you the first time complaining of loneliness and relationship problems. She relies on daydreams or fantasy to relieve boredom, and admits she does not want to grow up and leave the protection of her "pretend world." She would also like to learn how to be a better parent. She has made some impressive gains in her ability to parent her son more effectively, but remains lonely and restless.

Special Issues

There are some significant differences that need consideration in programming for female addicts. Many women do not seek treatment because they must care for their children. In our society, chemically dependent women are also considered more deviant than men who abuse drugs, making it difficult for women to seek treatment.

There is evidence to suggest that the vulnerability of children of alcoholics extends into adulthood. From a research standpoint, however, the evidence is less conclusive, and makes our understanding of the emotional and behavioral patterns of children who grow up in alcoholic homes less predictable than practice wisdom has suggested.

The client's concern about boredom and her adherence to her fantasy world are of concern. For clients who have lived "on the edge," entering a more balanced, healthier way of life can feel empty and boring by comparison. Monica could be in danger of relapse. Given the relationship that has been established, this is not an area the worker can ignore. Some confrontation may be indicated.

Key Concepts and Principles

Recovery
> In the field of chemical dependency this term connotes more than abstinence. It refers to an active process of working to heal and grow as a person.

Gender issues
> This concept is a reminder to individualize clients by not assuming that the masculine is the norm and not applying treatment strategies from that general bias. Valuing the feminine perspective is central to working with this population.

Suggested Activities

1. List the environmental or situational factors that may represent obstacles for this client.

2. Develop a list of questions to mutually assess the client's parenting skills. Evaluate the lists for cultural or value laden bias.

3. Role play a session in which the worker addresses Monica's boredom and loneliness. Avoid suggesting and advice giving.

4. Write in a journal thoughts and feelings about people known or suspected to be chemically addicted. Some possible questions to answer: Have you struggled with an addiction to caffeine, nicotine, sugar, food, alcohol, or other drugs? Have you had someone you love become addicted? What was the impact on you? Are your feelings about these areas of your life an asset to you in working with chemically addicted or dependent clients? Why or why not?

5. Design a policy for an agency or program that is based on the special needs of addicted women.

References and Recommended Reading

Blume, S. (1992). Alcohol and other drug problems in women. In J. Lowinson (Ed.), *Substance abuse: A comprehensive textbook* (pp. 794-806). Baltimore, MD: Williams and Wilkins.

Miller, W., & Baca, J. (1995). What every mental health professional should know about alcohol. *Journal of Substance Abuse and Treatment, 12*(5), 355-365.

Nelson-Zlupko, L., Kauffman, E., & Dore, M. M. (1995). Gender differences in drug addiction and treatment: Implications for social work intervention with substance-abusing women. *Social Work, 40*, 65-74.

Van Den Bergh, N. (Ed.). (1991). *Feminist perspectives on addictions.* New York: Springer.

A Change of Heart

The Agency

You are a social worker with the Department of Children's Services. You have been asked to evaluate both of the families in this case through a home study. This information will be used in resolving the conflict in this adoptive case. Agencies involved: Department of Children's Services, Children's Home Society, Juvenile Court System, U.S. Bureau of Indian Affairs, U.S. Congress, National Association of American Indian Social Workers, two law firms, the Indian Tribal Judges' Association, and the attorney who secured relinquishment.

The Client System

Billy (age 18) and Rachel (age 17), a Native American couple, eloped from their desert reservation to live together in a large city. Although naive and inexperienced, both found work. Unfortunately, earnings were scarcely enough to meet the expenses of big city living. Soon after, Rachel became pregnant and the couple was scared and confused. They believed they could not afford a child and were determined not to go back to the reservation. During the last month of pregnancy, they decided to respond to an adoption advertisement by a private attorney. According to the couple, they signed papers, received a check for $1,500 and an assurance that the hospital expenses would be paid by the attorney's office.

Rachel delivered twin girls whom she saw briefly following delivery. Within the next year economics improved for the couple, Rachel delivered a son, and the couple wanted the twin girls back. The couple returned to the reserva-

tion to ask for help from the tribe in getting the girls back. Tribal Council and family leaders held a meeting that lasted several days, and in the end, agreed that the attorney had taken advantage of the young couple, who had no right to sign away the children without tribal consent. The tribe in question considers children as members from birth regardless of blood degree. Although the tribe was poor, the consensus was to take out a loan to pay an Indian child welfare attorney in the city to rule the adoption invalid.

The twins are now 18 months old and have been traced to a wealthy, white couple with two older biological children. The final adoption decree has not been issued, and the tribal attorney filed a petition to have the adoption set aside. The angry adoptive parents countered by hiring a law firm to fight the case, and also enlisted the help of an influential congressman who began drafting amendments to the Indian Child Welfare Act (ICWA) in favor of the adoptive parents. The judge engaged a Native American psychologist and social worker to evaluate both families. The media called attention to the "Modern Indian War" and national interest was turned to the case. Hearings are pending.

Special Issues

Individuals who leave the reservation for the first time are often naive and vulnerable. Indian child welfare laws apply to adoption and custody cases if the child is a member of the tribe or eligible for membership. No state can place an Indian child in a non-Indian adoptive home without proper notice to the tribe and parents. Tribal jurisdiction takes precedence under rule of local domicile even when an Indian child is born off the reservation. Under ICWA, a tribe may have the adoption of an Indian child by non-Indians set aside, regardless of the number of years in the adoptive home so long as the final adoption decree has not been filed. During the 1940s, 1950s, and 1960s, Indian children were routinely removed from Indian families by well-meaning social workers who believed the children would be better off if reared in white homes. This oppressive and discriminatory policy was changed when the ICWA was established, and Native Americans were given opportunities to reverse enforced multi-ethnic adoptions.

Key Concepts and Principles

Oppression and discrimination

The social act of placing severe restrictions on an individual, group, or institution. Typically a government or political organization that is in power places these restrictions formally or covertly on oppressed groups so that they may be exploited or less able to compete with other social groups (Barker, 1999).

Social policy

The activities and principles of a society that guide the way it intervenes in and regulates relationships between individuals, groups, communities, and social institutions. These principles and activities are the result of society's values and customs and largely determine the distribution of resources and level of well-being of its people (Barker, 1999).

Suggested Activities

1. Using the problem solving process, role play an interview between a social worker and Billy and Rachel during the months in the city when Rachel was pregnant. Debrief and discuss the obstacles this couple faced in light of their individual development, marital relationship, and American Indian heritage.

2. Role play an interview between a social worker and Billy and Rachel three years later as they describe their feelings of grief and look back on their earlier decision. Debrief with those who role played and have the group discuss their reactions. Discuss the importance of the social worker's sensitivity to the Indian background of the couple and how this might be reflected in an interview.

3. Divide the class into small groups. Each group represents a "Friend of the Court Social Worker" and discusses recommendations for the presiding judge about which couple would make the better parents for the twin girls. Discuss and explore the different points of view.

4. Role play an interview between the adoptive parents and a social worker regarding their views, feelings, and desires about the children and the natural parents.

5. Research the various Native American tribes/nations located in this country. Discuss whether interventions would be different based on the different cultures.

6. Back to the Future Exercise. From the perspective of hindsight, identify points of potential intervention where a social worker may have been helpful in this situation. Discuss how this might have happened and the obstacles that prevented it.

7. Assign Hollingsworth (1998). Divide the group and hold a debate regarding same-race adoption vs. multi-ethnic adoption for children of color.

References and Recommended Reading

Barker, R. L. (1999). *The social work dictionary* (4th ed.). Washington, DC: NASW Press.

Ewalt, P., Freeman, E., Fortune, A., Poole, D., & Witkin, S. (Eds.). (1999). *Multicultural issues in social work: practice and research*. Washington, DC: NASW Press.

Goodluck, C., & Eckstein F. (1978). American Indian adoption program: An ethnic approach to child welfare. *White Cloud Journal, 1*, 3-7.

Hollingsworth, L. D. (1998). Promoting same race adoption for children of color. *Social Work, 43*, 104-116.

Sheafor, B., Horejsi, C. R., & Horejsi, G. (1997). *Techniques and guidelines for social work practice* (4th ed.). Needham Heights, MA: Allyn and Bacon.

Unit III

The Ending Phase: Best Laid Plans

Chapter 12

Integrating Change and Acknowledging Gains

A process by which the worker summarizes and incorporates the gains made by the client into the next phase of intervention.

All in the Family—Part II

(Refer to All in the Family—Part I in Chapter 3)

The Agency

The Sprucewood Mental Health Center is a state-run agency serving individuals and families of all ages. The center has a special program that focuses on the needs and problems of adolescents. The teen program offers individual treatment, as well as support groups for males and females. As a social worker in the teen program, you provide individual treatment and make referrals to support groups and to other workers.

The Client System

Jessica Smith (age 15) is an attractive white high school sophomore. She reports that she is happy with the way her second year of high school is going. She is a slim and athletic junior varsity cheerleader who is popular among her peers, brings home good grades, and is beginning to date.

The first meeting with you, the social worker, was an anxiety-producing experience for Jessica because you asked her many questions about her family, friends, school, and herself. Jessica was uncomfortable with the questions, and provided short answers designed to give the message "everything is fine with me." Jessica denied that she had a problem with food or her body image. Although Jessica didn't like talking about these things, she did like you, and agreed to come back for another session.

The second meeting went well, and Jessica continued to see you on a weekly basis. She shared her anger toward her parents, the pressure she felt to be perfect, and how she wished her older brother, Mike, would go to college so that she didn't have to be the one to do everything he didn't. In short, she felt resentful of Mike and her parents for placing the responsibility on her to be the "good child." Jessica said she "didn't feel she was perfect in any way," and as a result, felt out of control about her life. Jessica reluctantly admitted that she felt powerful when she engaged in self-induced vomiting, but still didn't "see why it was such a big deal." However, she agreed to family therapy and an eating disorders support group.

In the first meeting with the family, members discussed what they believed to be the problem and how they felt about coming in for treatment. Mr. Smith and Mike felt they had no reason to be present; they felt that Jessica should work on her own problems. Millie, Jessica's eight-year-old sister, didn't understand why she needed to be present, and Jessica was embarrassed to have to share her concerns with them. Only Jessica's mother seemed relieved that they were all there to "cure" Jessica's eating disorder. Jessica disclosed to her family that she is trying to figure out why she feels so much pressure at home.

Special Issues

A social worker assigned to the Smith family would want to have thorough knowledge of common communication problems that occur in families, in addition to age-related developmental tasks associated with each family member.

Key Concepts and Principles

Eating disorders

Severe disturbances in eating behavior that are accompanied by distorted perception of body shape and weight. Anorexia is characterized by a refusal to maintain a minimally normal body weight, and bulimia is defined by repeated binge eating and purging.

Family systems theory

Theory that emphasizes reciprocal relationships and mutual influence between individual family members and the whole and vice versa (Barker, 1999).

Suggested Activities

1. Role play a situation in which the worker(s) help the family talk about what each of their reactions to pressure/stress are, in order to understand why their current dynamics are contributing to Jessica's eating disorder. The workers may decide to continue working with the whole family, or with different groupings of family members as they see fit. Consider using solution-focused or structural family therapy models as the guiding framework.

2. Using systems theory as a framework, evaluate the Smith family and devise possible goals for change.

3. Invite a social worker to class to share their experiences in working with families.

4. Role play the first session of a teen eating disorders support group, using two social workers to work with a group of teen girls.

References and Recommended Reading

Barker, R. L. (1999). *The social work dictionary* (4th ed.). Washington, DC: NASW Press.

Franklin, C., & Jordan, C. (1999). *Family practice: Brief systems methods for social work.* Pacific Grove, CA: Brooks/Cole.

Gilligan, C. (1982). *In a different voice: Psychological theory and women's development.* Cambridge, MA: Harvard University Press.

Lukas, S. (1993). *Where to start and what to ask: An assessment handbook.* New York: Norton.

Minuchin, S., & Fishman, H. C. (1981). *Family therapy techniques.* Cambridge, MA: Harvard University Press.

Pipher, M. (1994). *Reviving Ophelia: Saving the selves of adolescent girls.* New York: Ballantine.

Thompson, J. K. (1996). *Body image, eating disorders, and obesity: An integrative guide for assessment and treatment.* Washington, DC: American Psychological Association.

Hard to Forget

The Agency

Whispering Elms is a private for-profit nursing facility located in a suburban area. Approximately 150 residents live in the facility, which serves a variety of ethnic and income groups from a three-county area. Residents have various diagnoses requiring 24-hour nursing care. The administrative staff consists of the administrator, director of nursing, dietary supervisor, maintenance supervisor, an activity director and one social worker.

The Client System

Greta (age 65) is a white female, widowed, with three adult children, Frederick, Harold, and Susan. All three, although engaged in full-time professions and married with adolescent children of their own, have been devoted to their mother. Greta has liver cancer and has about six months more to live. You, the social worker, have been asked by Greta to meet with her and the family regarding her final wishes and a living will. During the meeting it is apparent the children are uncomfortable, especially when talking about artificial hydration and nutrition. Greta starts talking about her funeral. Greta and her husband purchased "drawers" at the Jewish cemetery in a nearby area. Crying, she mentions that she assumes that all of the family will be buried near one another at the same Jewish cemetery. Harold states that he and his wife have decided to be cremated when they die. Greta yells, "How can you allow yourself to be cremated after what Hitler and his thugs did to our people? How can any Jew be cremated after Hitler's ovens?" She tells everyone to leave the room. Frederick,

Harold, and Susan are visibly upset. Harold regrets bringing up his views on cremation. Frederick cannot understand his mother's point of view and says, "The Holocaust ended more than 50 years ago." Susan reminds him that their grandfather (Greta's father) died in the gas chambers of Auschwitz. They tell you that they are worried their mother might refuse to speak to them for weeks or months, and she might not have weeks or months left to live.

Special Issues

End-of-life decision making can be stressful for the family as well as for the individual making his/her wishes known. This case is further complicated by a conflict of values among the family members. The social worker's first responsibility is to the resident, supporting her in her right to complete advance directives (e.g., living will, treatment decisions, durable power of attorney for health care). The social worker also has a responsibility to work with the family of the resident, either individually or as a group, establishing boundaries to preserve the confidentiality of all persons. Various social work roles are relevant in this case (counselor, advocate, group facilitator, educator), and it is important to assume each role in a deliberate manner with an understanding of the parameters of each.

Key Concepts and Principles

Advance directives

A properly witnessed and documented statement that describes in detail the medical measures a person would or would not want used when no longer able to make such measures known. The document may also name a surrogate who could make such decisions for the individual.

Values clarification

A method of education in moral and ethical principles that occurs by bringing together people to share their opinions and value perspectives. This exposes the participants to different ideals and permits them to appreciate the relative nature of values.

Suggested Activities

1. Obtain blank copies of your state's Living Will for each student. Ask students to fill out the documents to have some understanding of the process clients go through when completing advance directives (Important: to preserve student rights, the documents are not to be signed or witnessed and students may destroy them after completing the exercise). Discuss reactions to the exercise.

2. Contact a local synagogue or Jewish social services organization for a speaker on Jewish history and heritage.

3. View portions of one of the films dealing with the Holocaust (e.g., *Schindler's List*) and discuss it in class.

4. Role play a subsequent meeting with Greta and her family, assuming they have all agreed to a family meeting with you to discuss Greta's wishes regarding her end-of-life decisions.

References and Recommended Reading

Bullis, R. K. (1996). *Spirituality in social work practice*. Bristol, PA: Taylor and Francis.

Hersen, M., & Van Hasselt, V. B. (Eds.). (1998). *Handbook of clinical geropsychology*. New York: Plenum.

Loewenberg, F. M., & Dolgoff, R. (1996). *Ethical decisions for social work practice* (5th ed.). Itasca, IL: F. E. Peacock.

Chapter 13

Anticipating the End/The Final Session

Because professional relationships are purposeful and finite, the ending should be a reality from the beginning to enhance goal clarity and worker role definition. The termination phase should provide opportunity for affirmation and integration of past work, sharing feelings about the loss of an important relationship, and preparation for the future.

Movin' On Out

The Agency

The Passages Agency is set up to serve the needs of teenagers in foster care or high risk neighborhoods who either have become emancipated at very young ages or who are preparing for independent living after foster care. Youth who enroll in the program are allocated $5.00 for travel money to the weekly psychoeducational groups designed to teach specific knowledge and skills to help them make a smooth transition to independent living. Money management, job interviewing, resume preparation, nutrition, good work habits, health, and safe sex are among the topics that are covered over an eight week period. The agency is funded by private donations, grants, and United Way. It has nonprofit status and an excellent reputation in the community for providing quality services. Individual counseling or case management is offered to group members only in special circumstances.

The Client System

Angela (age 15) is a Hispanic single mother of a three-month-old baby girl. She dropped out of high school when she became pregnant at the beginning of her freshman year, and is now living below the poverty line. She and the baby move back and forth between living with her boyfriend (age 18) or her mother, depending on whether or not Angela and her boyfriend are getting along. Angela experiences her mother as overly controlling. Angela believes her mother tries to tell her how to live her life and also tries to parent her child. A primary source of tension between Angela and her boyfriend is his lack of employment and her perception that he is not trying very hard

to find a job. He, like Angela, never completed high school but does have a General Equivalency Diploma. Angela would prefer to be totally independent from her mother, and ideally, she would like to move out of her family's house permanently. At the present time, Angela is living with her boyfriend and his family—her boyfriend's mother, his sister and her two children—in a small house located in a high risk (for crime, health problems, and lack of adequate day care) neighborhood. Angela has no job skills, but seems to be very intelligent and has a strong motivation to learn.

Although Angela has few ties with her neighbors, she has one close friend and is close to a sister in another state who helps out financially when she can. Angela dreams about going back to school and getting a good job, but feels torn because she does not like the idea of leaving her young daughter.

As the agency social worker, you met Angela when she joined the group you facilitate. Because she was pregnant at the time, you extended individual services to her for three months before the baby was born. You have seen her individually or in group once a week since then. There are four weeks remaining before you leave the agency, and you are therefore faced with bringing closure to an important relationship with many issues unresolved and many needs still unmet.

Special Issues

As is often the case when confronted with a complex client situation in which there are many needs and limited resources, it is difficult to think of closure in any final sense. At least one issue in this case is the importance of making conscious use of the last few weeks of the relationship and thinking about how the final session can be made the most meaningful for the client. This should be done keeping in mind such things as the client's history of previous losses, her strong investment in becoming independent, her age, her responsibility as a parent, and the extent of her identification with her heritage.

Related to the above is the need to think with Angela of creative ways to help her receive more positive support so she can rely less on her critical mother, and at the same time begin to realize some of her personal dreams related to returning to school.

Key Concepts and Principles

Teen parenting

Providing the concrete and emotional resources to meet the challenges of parenthood to parents who are children themselves is an enormous challenge. Nonjudgmental respect is crucial.

Ethnic identity

The extent to which one claims and identifies with his/her traditional ethnic heritage.

Social work roles

Classic social work roles include facilitator, counselor or therapist, mediator, advocate, broker, case manager, planner, educator.

Suggested Activities

1. Role play the worker introducing the topic of termination for the first time with Angela, a subsequent session with the last session soon approaching, and the final session in which the worker says good-bye to Angela.

2. In small groups, discuss ways of ending time together with a person or persons for whom you care a great deal, with casual acquaintances, and with strangers. Recall how you leave or might leave different people at the airport. Would you be more likely to drop them off at the curb? Walk them to the gate? Wave until you can no longer see the plane in the sky?

3. Individually, reflect on meaningful good-bye(s) in life by answering the following: What made them so significant? What was helpful and not so helpful in the process? What does this teach you about how you would like for your clients to experience endings with you? What can you do to enhance that process? Share ideas with the whole class.

4. Individually, select a piece of music, a poem, a sculpture or a painting that is a partial reflection of your feelings when you experience change, loss, or a good-bye to someone or something that you love. Share it with the class.

5. Suggest a macro strategy for helping to prevent teen pregnancy. Give your rationale and be able to defend your proposal.

References and Recommended Reading

Hawkins, J. D., Catalano, R. F., Kosterman, R., Abbott, R., & Hill, K. G. (1999). Preventing adolescent health-risk behaviors and strengthening protection during childhood. *Archives of Pediatrics and Adolescent Medicine, 153*, 226-234.

Kirby, D. (1999). Reflections on two decades of research on teen sexual behavior and pregnancy. *Journal of School Health, 69*, 89-104.

Resnick, M. D., Bearman, P. S., & Blum, R.W. (1997). Protecting adolescents from harm: Findings from the National Longitudinal Study on Adolescent Health. *JAMA, 278*(10), 823.

Sheafor, B., Horejsi, C. R., & Horejsi, G. (1997) Termination of service. In *Techniques and guidelines for social work practice* (4th ed., pp. 600-602). Needham Heights, MA: Allyn and Bacon.

Saying Goodbye

The Agency

You are a social worker at Mountain Oaks, a "continuum of care" campus for older adults located in a suburban area. The campus consists of independent apartments, an assisted living facility, and a nursing home. The agency prides itself on providing care for older adults throughout all life transitions experienced by its residents. It is a church-affiliated agency and provides care regardless of a client's ability to pay for services or religious affiliation.

The Client System

Mr. Jackson (age 72) is an alert and oriented white male who is living in one of the apartments at Mountain Oaks. He has thick gray hair, a tanned complexion, muscular, but lean build, and erect posture. Although he has Parkinson's Disease, it does not significantly impair his mobility at this time. He and his wife have been married for 50 years and experienced the sudden death of their 47-year-old only child, John, six months ago. John never married, and there are no grandchildren. However, a number of nieces and nephews live in the immediate area. Mr. Jackson is a retired military officer and has a substantial retirement income. His wife was hospitalized three days ago for routine surgery and was to be discharged from the hospital yesterday. A niece planned to bring Mrs. Jackson to the couple's apartment since Mr. Jackson no longer drives. Mr. Jackson was awaiting his wife's arrival when he received a phone call from the hospital chaplain informing him that his wife had unexpectedly died from a massive stroke. The body was cremated the same day, and there are no plans for a funeral or memorial service. Tearfully, Mr. Jackson states that his marriage "is a friendship as well as a marriage. We have always enjoyed each other's company. I can't imagine life without her. She is my rock." Later, he says, "I never even got to say good-bye to her and tell her how much I love her." The administrator of Mountain Oaks contacted you, the social worker, to meet with Mr. Jackson the day before he is moving from your facility to live with a brother and sister-in-law. You met with the Jacksons when they first arrived at the facility approximately a year ago and you have been meeting with them regularly following the death of their son.

Special Issues

Depression is the most prevalent mental health problem in adults over the age of 65 and is often undiagnosed or misdiagnosed. Recently widowed, older adult white males represent the highest risk for depression, suicide, or both. Additionally, the client is still actively grieving his son's death. Mr. Jackson has Parkinson's Disease, which appears to be in an early stage. Since this is a progressive disease, it is expected to worsen, especially with the onset of stressful events. There is a lack of closure for Mr. Jackson since his wife's death was unexpected and there were no death rituals (e.g., funeral, memorial service, graveside ceremony). The social worker's grief and loss are also an issue since Mrs. Jackson was a client and there was an ongoing therapeutic relationship prior to her death. In addition, Mr. Jackson is moving from the area, thus terminating the relationship.

Key Concepts and Principles

Grief work

A series of emotional stages or phases following an important loss, which gradually permit adjustment and recovery. The individual typically reminisces, expresses emotions, accepts, adjusts to the new situation, and forms new relationships.

Developmental approach

An orientation toward or focus on the predictable changes that occur throughout the human life cycle, including physical, mental, social, and environmental changes.

Unplanned termination

Discontinuing services to clients who are still in need but for whom circumstances such as moving away from service area preclude continued involvement by the same worker.

Gerontological social work

An orientation and specialization in social work concerned with the psychosocial treatment of older adults—the development and management of needed social services and programs for older individuals.

Suggested Activities

1. Role play the final meeting with Mr. Jackson, paying attention to unresolved issues.

2. Apply the Kubler-Ross stages of grief and loss to Mr. Jackson.

3. List the resources available to Mr. Jackson.

4. Role play a client-worker interaction exploring the ways in which Mr. Jackson might bring closure regarding his wife's death.

5. Discuss possible grief and loss issues relevant to the social worker.

6. Develop an outline for a program for the agency to adopt in support of residents who are grieving.

References and Recommended Reading

Butler, R. N., Lewis, M. I., & Sunderland, T. (1998). *Aging and mental health: Positive psychosocial and biomedical approaches* (5th ed.). Needham Heights, MA: Allyn and Bacon.

Hersen, M., & Van Hasselt, V. B. (Eds.). (1998). *Handbook of clinical geropsychology.* Needham Heights, MA: Allyn and Bacon.

Johnson, H. W. (1998). *The social services: An introduction* (5th ed.). Itasca, IL: F. E. Peacock.

Unit IV

Special Issues: Exceptions to the Rule

Chapter 14

Values and Ethics

The Social Work Code of Ethics is an explicit statement of the values, principles, and rules of the social work profession, which regulates the conduct of its members. The NASW Code of Ethics applies to all social workers who are members of the National Association of Social Workers. Six core social work values are inherent in the National Association of Social Workers Code of Ethics: (1) service, (2) social justice, (3) dignity and worth of persons, (4) importance of human relationships, (5) integrity, and (6) competence.

Ethical Potpourri

The Agency

The agency provides early childhood intervention services for children with disabilities and their caregivers. The agency is situated in the center of an African-American community, but services are provided to a county-wide area that includes approximately 250,000 residents, most from minority backgrounds. The median age of caregivers is 23, and the average household income is $18,000. All services are provided on a sliding fee scale. Staff is diverse in terms of ethnicity and disability. While the social service staff includes bachelor's-level workers, the education staff includes bachelor's-level instructors and two supervisors. One supervisor has a graduate degree in special education; the other has a graduate degree in public health education.

The Client System

Scenario #1: The BSW interns have brought you, their field instructor, a request from one of their classroom instructors who is interested in using current agency clientele to ascertain the type of problems faced by African-American parents of children with disabilities.

Scenario #2: As one of the social workers, you come face to face with a client at the grocery store. The client shows nonverbal acknowledgment.

Scenario #3: You make an initial visit to a couple who has recently sought services. The couple is from another country and struggling with pressure from the pediatrician who referred them for services. As the interview progresses to problem identification it becomes clear that the couple is struggling with the expectation that they will give priority to the survival of their child. In their belief system, children with disabilities should be kept as comfortable as possible, but death is expected and considered to be a natural outcome that should not be questioned.

Scenario #4: After three and a half years of service, a social worker is showing signs of "compassion fatigue" as evidenced by his generalizations about parents and staff members of other agencies in the agency's cachment area. In a staff meeting you just attended, he made several negative references to the single parent and health nurse involved in one of his cases. He followed the statement by saying that such behaviors could only be expected from uneducated caregivers and uncaring health providers. This particular social worker is one who has been in the field many years. He is also well recognized in this field and has a good reputation in the community.

Special Issues

Some of the families with whom the agency works may include caregivers who do not speak English, and some of them may also have belief systems that differ from those of the general population and the staff. Additional issues included in these scenarios are those of confidentiality and social workers' need to be aware of their own possible compassion fatigue or other signs of stress.

Key Concepts and Principles

Cultural competency
  The necessity for a social worker to be knowledgeable about differing needs and

values among diverse clients, including how to work with clients regarding specific ethnic and acculturation issues.

Suggested Activities

1. Review the NASW Code of Ethics. How does the code apply to each of the scenarios?
2. Role play scenario#1. The field instructor and the student present the request to the agency director and a specific idea on how outcome evaluation could serve the agency's assurance goals as well as the university's interest in developing long term research on persons with disabilities.
3. Role play scenario #2. Simulate the grocery store chance meeting.
4. Role play scenario #3. Simulate a follow-up visit to the home of a couple who does not believe that medical intervention is necessary for the disability of their infant child.
5. Role play scenario #4. Confront the staff member who is making negative and stereotyping remarks about agency clientele and some of the other agency professional staff.

References and Recommended Reading

Hepworth, D. H., Rooney, R. H., & Larsen, J. A. (1997). *Direct social work practice: Theory and skills* (5th ed.). Pacific Grove, CA: Brooks/Cole.

Leigh, J. W. (1998). *Communicating for cultural competence.* Needham Heights, MA: Allyn and Bacon.

Loewenberg, F. M., & Dolgoff, R. (1996). *Ethical decisions for social work practice* (5th ed.). Itasca, IL: F. E. Peacock.

Honesty Is the Best Policy

The Agency

You are a social worker in a private, for-profit agency that provides counseling services to individuals, couples, and families. Most of the clientele come from a middle-class white background with insurance benefits that allow for mental health services. The agency is comprised of a psychiatrist, psychologist, and several social workers who have their advanced practice credentials and are licensed at the highest level. You are currently supervised by one of the agency's senior social workers.

The Client System

You have been working with a married couple both of whom are in their late-twenties, white, childless, and involved in separate careers. They have indicated a desire to improve the quality of their relationship. Direct, open, and honest communication has been agreed upon as a relationship goal. Each has also expressed that sexual fidelity is an important dimension of their marriage. The sessions have been characterized by completed "homework" assignments on couples' communication and a reported increase in sexual intimacy. Between the fourth and fifth meetings, you receive a telephone call from one of the partners who says, "I think it would help you to know that I am involved romantically with another person. It does not affect my relationship with my spouse, and I feel quite sure you will not reveal this information. I want you to know because I respect your expertise and surely you can work around this situation. You are doing a wonderful job."

Special Issues

The importance of contracting between the couple and worker is evident in this case. With a good contract, the ethics and values of the social worker are made clear as far as the therapeutic relationship is concerned. The value of boundaries and recognition of personal values are also important.

Key Concepts and Principles

Social work boundaries
Invisible lines of demarcation which circumscribe the area of the client and worker relationship based on, but not limited to: ethics, values, professional use of self, social work roles, and nature of the helping relationship.

Social work supervision
An administrative and educational process used extensively in agencies to help social workers further develop and refine their skills and to provide quality assurance for clients (Barker, 1999).

Suggested Activities

1. Role play the social worker's response to the unfaithful spouse.
2. Role play the social worker's response to the other spouse.
3. Examine the NASW Social Work Code of Ethics to determine what portion(s) address this situation.

4. Discuss the aspects of contracting in couples counseling.

5. Discuss the common assumption that the unfaithful spouse is a male even though the vignette does not specify which person contacted the worker to reveal the extramarital relationship.

6. Discuss the value of professional supervision in this situation. How does it differ from professional consultation?

References and Recommended Reading

Barker, R. L. (1999). *The social work dictionary* (4th ed.). Washington, DC: NASW Press.

Linzer, N. (1999). *Resolving ethical dilemmas in social work practice*. Needham Heights, MA: Allyn and Bacon.

Loewenberg, F. M., & Dolgoff, R. (1996). *Ethical decisions for social work practice* (5th ed.). Itasca, IL: F. E. Peacock.

Chapter 15

Diverse Populations

The differences among groups of individuals including differences in age, gender, sexual orientation, spiritual orientation, culture, ethnicity, and race.

A Stranger in a Strange Land

The Agency

The agency is in a large public high school on the periphery of an exploding and rapidly changing metropolitan area. The school reflects the conservative attitudes of the nearby rural communities and where there is fear of anything that is "foreign," governmental, or challenging to the ethnocentrism of the locale. Most of the people in the neighborhoods are poor, working-class, or unemployed. Ethnically the school is about 50% Hispanic, 25% African American, and 25% white. There are two school social workers and two high school counselors for 1500 students. The counselors function more as assistant principals, and the school social worker's mandate is to work with students "at risk" for academic failure who are referred by school personnel. As a school social worker you are assigned to this school two days each week for the academic year. The remaining workdays are divided between two other schools.

The Client System

Ted (age 15) is an African-American freshman male. He was referred to the school social workers by his teacher in the second six weeks of school when she noticed that Ted's grades and concentration were poor. Ted had an excellent academic record prior to this year. He was enrolled in honor classes, had a passion for the theatre, and a wonderful sense of humor. Lately, however, his teacher sensed that he might be depressed, was aware that he seemed to be alone much of the time, and noticed that the other teens sometimes called him names.

Ted lives alone with his mother. He has a brother and a father who live in another part of the state. Ted and his mother moved to their current home when Ted was in the sixth grade. Ted disclosed his homosexuality to his mother last year, and she has been supportive of him in his struggle to be who he is in a homophobic school culture. Ted's father is very conservative and religious. Fearing his father's total rejection, Ted has not come out to his father. Ted was first seen by the school social worker who is your supervisor. He reported that Ted was having difficulty sleeping and getting out of bed in the morning, and that he was unable to concentrate. Ultimately, Ted had threatened suicide. A suicide contract had been signed at that time, and his mother had agreed to make an appointment for him to be evaluated for antidepressant medication. Your supervisor subsequently assigned this case to you.

Ted revealed to you that much of his unhappiness, anger, and low self-esteem are the result of his daily experiences at the high school. Food and drink are thrown at him during lunch, he is called degrading names, and laughed at while walking through the halls between classes. A second concern of Ted's is his mother's return to drinking. Communication between them has seriously deteriorated over the last several months.

Special Issues

Developmental tasks of adolescence are complicated for homosexual teens, especially in an environment that is prejudiced against gays and lesbians. Ted is at serious risk for bodily harm, self-inflicted, as well as from the rampant homophobia in the school.

Many gay/lesbian teens have inaccurate information about gay or lesbian sex, no gay or lesbian role models, and no safe place where they talk about confusing feelings. Ted had no knowledge of any other homosexuals at school, so his sense of isolation was profound.

Finally, it may be dangerous for a teenager to reveal his/her sexual orientation to parents. They may feel that they have failed their parents. A teenager's coming out may place him/herself in jeopardy and the family in crisis. The issue of whether to come out, how, and to whom, is extremely sensitive.

Key Concepts and Principles

Coming out

The process of self-identification as a lesbian or a gay man, followed by revelation of one's sexual orientation to others (Barker, 1999).

Homophobia

The fear of homosexuals and homosexuality. A related concept is heterosexism, which is the belief that heterosexuality is normative and that non-heterosexuality is deviant and intrinsically less desirable (Berkman & Zinberg, 1997).

Professional use of self

The management of worker values, beliefs, and feelings to the benefit of clients. It is more than simply not allowing one's own agenda to interfere with the work with clients—it also suggests having a responsibility to use values, beliefs, and feelings effectively.

Suggested Activities

1. Role play a teenager coming out to the social worker. Discuss feelings on the part of the client and the worker.

2. Invite gay men and lesbians from the community to share their experiences growing up homosexual and something about what their lives are like now.

3. Reflect in writing about working with gays and lesbians. What do you need to work on in order to be more comfortable with this population? How can you begin to get help to be more effective? What would you like to see addressed in this class? (These notes will be anonymous, but will be turned in to the instructor who will generalize from them and share them with the class for discussion.)

4. Research the Web for articles to share with the class on the ways adolescence is experienced by gay and lesbian teenagers including suicidality, substance abuse and homelessness.

5. As the school social worker, what changes in school policy would you recommend to the principal? To the school board?

References and Recommended Reading

Barker, R. L. (1999). *The social work dictionary* (4th edition). Washington, DC: NASW Press.

Berkman, C. S., & Zinberg, G. (1997). Homophobia and heterosexism in social workers. *Social Work, 42*, 319-332.

Hersch, P. (1991). Secret lives. *The Family Networker.* January/February, 37-43.

Lukes, C., & Land, H. (1990). Biculturality and homosexuality. *Social Work, 35*, 155-161.

Markowitz, L. M. (1991). Homosexuality: Are we still in the dark? *The Family Networker.* January/ February 27-29.

Exploring Beyond the Surface

The Agency

The agency is the student services department in a publicly funded small community college. A psychologist is the chief administrator of the department, which includes a staff member with a masters in education and one social worker. In addition to helping students with regular academic and administrative problems, the staff assist students to take full advantage of the career and personal counseling services available. Long term counseling, both group and individual, crisis intervention, problem solving, and referral are all available to any student enrolled in the college.

The Client System

Suma (age 28) is an Indian woman who came to the student advisor's office seeking information about transferring credits from a former university. She speaks with a very heavy Indian accent and struggles with the English language. As the social worker, you recognized signs of exhaustion and frustration in Suma and gave her information about the services in the student advisor's office, which included counseling and referral for specific needs.

Suma indicated that she has recently separated from her husband, who has returned to India, leaving Suma to raise three children, ages six, eight, and eleven. She has been working full-time while trying to obtain a business degree. Most of her previous work was in another major so she needs help changing majors. This is another reason for her visit to the social worker's office.

Suma revealed that she has sought refuge at the local battered women's shelter, and has learned of several community resources to help her with her children; therefore, day care is not an issue at the present time. She admitted that she did not have the energy to grieve or feel angry about her husband's abuse of her and his ultimate abandonment of the family. For now, her focus is on survival, although she does have a goal of becoming an American citizen. She wants citizenship because she is in disgrace with her family for having been deserted by her husband and is no longer welcome in India. She is familiar with the Hindu Temple in town, but has had little time to participate in activities there.

Special Issues

This case illustrates a practice dilemma that social workers frequently encounter. When clients are already stretched very thin in trying to meet their everyday responsibilities, how does one help without burdening the client with yet another thing to do, place to go, paper to fill out, etc.?

A second issue involves the consideration of cultural values. It is important to assess the level of acculturation. In addition to dialogue with the client, dress, speech, and other nonverbal cues should be part of the assessment.

Key Concepts and Principles

Impact of cultural values on self-esteem
> The values of the dominant culture as well as traditional ethnic values can contribute to or erode individual self-esteem. Particularly relevant here is the impact of these and the client's sense of herself as a woman.

Acculturation

The degree to which an individual or family has been absorbed into the mainstream culture.

Referral process

Effective referral requires a great deal of knowledge and skill such as knowing client capacity for accessing resources, and how practical and accessible the resources really are. A good referral is much more than giving a client a number to call.

Suggested Activities

1. Visit an Asian restaurant, temple, or celebration in the community.
2. Discuss the worker's role and what the worker can offer the client.

3. Role play a subsequent interview with Suma where she returns for help and support when her husband and family pressure her to return her children to India.

4. Research policy issues regarding immigration and naturalization. How do these policies affect Suma? Suma's children?

References and Recommended Reading

Karnow, S., & Yoshihara, N. (1992). *Asian Americans in transition*. New York: The Asia Society.

Min, G. P. (1995). *Asian Americans: Contemporary trends and issues*. London: Sage.

Minault, G. (1986). *India 2000: The next fifteen years*. Riverdale, MD: New Delhi.

Roland, A. (1996). *Cultural pluralism and psychoanalysis*. New York: Routledge.

Sheafor, B. W., Horejsi, C. R., & Horejsi, G. A. (1997). *Techniques and guidelines for social work practice* (4th ed.). Needham Heights, MA: Allyn and Bacon.

Caught Between Two Fires

The Agency

You are a caseworker at Child Protective Services in a predominantly Native American part of the state. Your job is to provide protection to minor children when they are in danger of abuse, neglect, or abandonment. Often other agencies become involved as well, such as Legal Aid, the criminal justice system, state public welfare, Social Security Administration, school system, Family Court System, Indian Health Service, and potentially the Indian Tribal Court.

The Client System

Mrs. Harjo (age 65) is a Creek Indian widow and matriarch of the Harjo Bear Clan. She lives on Harjo Hill and subsists on Supplemental Security Income, food stamps, and her garden. The place name was bestowed by a rural post master many years ago and the entire Harjo extended family has lived and died on "the hill" for as long as local residents can remember.

A paternal grandson, Anthony "Tony" Door, Jr. (age 13), recently moved in with Mrs. Harjo following his mother's death from acute alcohol poisoning. Tony's biological father, Anthony Harjo, is currently serving five years in county jail on a third conviction. Tony's parents were never married, and his white mother never obtained a legal divorce from her first husband before becoming Anthony's common-law wife. When Tony was born, the hospital registrar listed the first husband as the legal father on his birth certificate. Nevertheless, the child was named for his biological father and called Tony.

Trying to do the right thing, Mrs. Harjo went to Tony's school to give notice of a change of address and to put her name on file as guardian and emergency contact. School officials pointed out that Tony was not legally related to Mrs. Harjo, and that therefore she had no authority to authorize medical care, or to enroll Tony in school. The principal referred Mrs. Harjo to Legal Aid where she appealed for help in getting Tony's paternity corrected. The attorney advised that Anthony adopt Tony in order to change the legal parent. However, Legal Aid refused to take the case because Tony's father was incarcerated, and because of his criminal record could not give a favorable home study. Moreover, the whereabouts of the legal father are unknown, and thus no relinquishment can be secured. Tony's aunts and uncles discussed adopting him and argued about the injustice of taking him away from his natural father thorough "white law." You, the social worker, are given the case to investigate.

Special Issues

In the Creek culture, families are extended, not nuclear. Traditional Creek kin groups do not interact with the dominant culture unless absolutely necessary. Decision making is a group process, and no action can be taken without consensus. The Indian Child Welfare Act (ICWA) does not apply to unwed fathers where paternity is not proven. If Creek ancestry comes through the unwed father, the tribe has no recourse under ICWA without a paternity determination. Creek children (males especially) often have serious problems with identity, especially if attending public schools as minority students.

Key Concepts and Principles

Empathy

> The ability to put oneself into the other's situation and understand the experience of "walking in their shoes."

Culturally sensitive social work practice

> The process of professional intervention while being knowledgeable, perceptive, empathic, and skillful about the unique as well as common characteristics of clients who possess racial, ethnic, religious, gender, age, sexual orientation, or socioeconomic differences (Barker, 1999).

Suggested Activities

1. Simulate an interagency meeting in which representatives from each of the agencies involved in the case come together to discuss possible resolutions. Students represent each agency and two of the family members (an aunt and uncle). Discuss the value, ethical, and legal considerations that arise during the session.

2. In small groups, brainstorm and then prioritize the issues and order of resolution to restore family functioning. Discuss as a larger group.

3. Role play an interview where Tony and his biological father each tell their story to a local newspaper reporter. Debrief the role play by discussing the various issues that impact these two people including loss of family, loss of freedom, loss of identity, and developmental issues.

4. Invite a member of the Creek tribe or another Native American tribe to speak to the class about their experiences with the white community, focusing especially on legal issues, lifestyle decisions, and the clash of cultural values.

References and Recommended Reading

Barker, R. L. (1999). *The social work dictionary* (4th ed.). Washington, DC: NASW Press.

Shulman, L. (1999). *The skills of helping individuals, families, groups, and communities.* Itasca, IL: F. E. Peacock.

Sue, D. W., & Sue, D. (1995). *Counseling the culturally different: Theory and practice* (2nd ed.). New York: John Wiley and Sons.

Sutton, C. E. T., & Nose, M. A. B. (1996). American Indian families: An overview. In M. McGoldrick, J. Giordano, & J. K. Pearce (Eds.), *Ethnicity and family therapy* (2nd ed., pp. 31-44). New York: Guilford.

Tafoya, N., & Vecchio, A. D. (1996). Back to the future: An examination of the Native American holocaust experience. In M. McGoldrick, J. Giordano, & J. K. Pearce (Eds.), *Ethnicity and family therapy* (2nd ed., pp. 45-54). New York: Guilford.

Wassinger, L. (1993). The value system of the Native American counseling client: An exploration. *American Indian Culture and Research Journal, 17*(4), 91-98.

Williams, E. E., & Ellison, F. (1999). Culturally informed social work practice with American Indian clients: Guidelines for non-Indian social workers. In P. L. Ewalt, E. M. Freeman, S. A. Kirk, & D. L. Poole (Eds.), *Multicultural issues in social work: Practice and research* (pp. 78-84). Washington DC: NASW Press.

Seeking Refuge

The Agency

You are a social worker within a small non-profit program for refugees and other immigrants who have recently arrived in a very densely populated inner-city neighborhood known as a *barrio* in the Southwest.

This particular *barrio* is approximately three miles from the international bridge leading to and from a Mexican city of approximately one million inhabitants. The cities on both sides of this border include manufacturing plants known as *maquiladoras* where apparel, household products, and motor vehicles are built under the international trade agreement known as NAFTA. Wages are low, and there are complaints among workers regarding gender and class discrimination encountered on the job sites. On the Mexican side, workers self advocate by joining workers' unions, *sindicatos*, while the workers on the American plants usually work within AFL-CIO programs to have their needs addressed.

Refugees from Central American countries often work in a Mexican border community before they can afford to buy their way into the United States. Work at the *maquiladoras*, therefore, is a welcome option. The same is true of migrants from the interior of Mexico.

Your job at this center is to provide family-oriented services for agency clientele. In addition to the "Closet & Pantry Services" which provide food and clothing for arriving families, you can access counseling and legal services on a pro bono basis from an extensive list of community volunteers. You also have access to leaders in the *sindicatos* and the AFL-CIO program for Spanish-speaking workers. Finally, The agency has a list of trained volunteers who can provide interpreter services.

The Client System

Olivia Madero (age 25), originally from El Salvador, arrives with a number of concerns.

You notice that she appears to be older than her age, and that her clothes seem to be for a much larger person. In addition, she has an unsightly rash on her arms, neck and legs. Her face is slightly flushed. Her features are clearly indigenous, and Spanish is her primary language.

Olivia was referred to the agency by a nun who volunteers at a health clinic for *maquiladora* workers across the border. The clinic had provided medical treatment for the rash, but the main concern was the sexual harassment that Olivia had encountered at the *maquiladoras*. Olivia tells you her life story which includes accounts of violence in El Salvador and her travels through the republic of Mexico. Her father was killed by the military in El Salvador. Her mother and older sisters were repeatedly raped. Her two brothers managed to escape through Mexico, but one died while being smuggled across the border. She now has a surviving brother in Chicago, her mother and older sisters in El Salvador, and various relatives scattered in Mexico.

During her employment in *las maquiladoras*, Olivia encountered two male supervisors who demanded sexual favors in return for better work shifts and higher wages. Her complaints in the *sindicatos* were not acknowledged. There were some very strong and assertive female leaders in the *sindicatos*, but their priorities were political and economical. Finally, Olivia saved enough money to pay a "coyote" (a smuggler) to bring her across to the United States and provide a work permit (green card), as well as a social security number with which to find employment. With her sewing skills, she quickly accessed employment in the United States *barrio*, but her lack of English language skills, and social isolation due to her illegal status, have now resulted in symptoms of depression.

Special Issues

Working on the Mexico-United States border presents situations not found in other parts of this country. Refugees, undocumented workers, and recent immigrants all present unique challenges for social work intervention. Language and culture can be possible barriers to effective service delivery. Political and economic situations provide further complications.

Key Concepts and Principles

Social policy

Social policies are rules by which the people in a society are expected to live. They also determine the allocation of resources and the nature of social programs and services (Kirst-Ashman & Hull, 1999).

Ethical dilemma

These dilemmas occur when the values of various systems clash and decisions must be made based on hierarchical determinations.

Suggested Activities

1. Divide into groups whose foci will be women's health, women's issues in border communities, sexual harassment on the job site, and refugees' legal and mental health issues. Discuss and formulate change goals that could possibly improve the future of women in these environments.

2. Divide into two groups. Role play group sessions as follows. One group is to role play a *sindicato* meeting in which Olivia and other *maquiladora* workers complain about sexual harassment on the job and demand the *sindicato* give priority to their concerns as quickly as possible.

a. Discuss the ethical dilemmas inherent in this scenario.

b. Role play a group session (in the same agency) to which Olivia and other immigrant women are invited to discuss women's issues. Olivia finally confides that she was repeatedly raped during her travel through Mexico. She often wonders if her exodus was worth the subsequent tribulations. Her sisters and mother are in El Salvador and have endured similar experiences; however, they are together. She, on the other hand, has endured much pain alone, and her entry to the United States carries both hope and much anxiety about the future.

3. Discuss worker secondary trauma. Olivia's story includes much violence. How can social workers deal with their own needs while responding in a prompt and competent manner to client needs?

4. Assign students to access Internet and library information regarding legalization of a refugee from Central America. Note the difference in resources available to immigrants from other parts of the world. Note the difference in resources available to refugees with protected status and those who simply arrive as illegal immigrants. On the basis of these findings, what are Olivia's opportunities, and what are the possible barriers to a legal immigration and naturalization process?

5. Invite a guest speaker who can share his or her story as a former refugee. Discuss how agencies can be sensitive and culturally competent for such clientele.

References and Recommended Reading

Falicov, C. J. (1998). *Latino families in therapy: A guide to multicultural practice.* New York: Guilford.

Kirst-Ashman, K. K., & Hull, H. H., Jr. (1999). *Understanding generalist practice* (2nd ed.). Chicago: Nelson-Hall.

Lecca, P. J., Quervalu, I., Nunes, J. V., & Gonzales, H. F. (1998). *Cultural competency in health, social, & human services: Directions for the twenty-first century.* New York: Garland.

Sue, D. W., Carter, R. T., Casas, J. M., Fouad, N. A., Ivey, A. E., Jensen, M., LaFromboise, T., Manese, J. E., Ponterotto, J. G., & Vasquez-Nutall, E. (1998). *Multicultural counseling competencies: Individual and organizational development.* Thousand Oaks, CA: Sage.

Toseland, R. W., & Rivas, R. F. (1998). *An introduction to group work practice* (3rd ed.). Needham Heights, MA: Allyn and Bacon.

Asia Elders

The Agency

This inner-city, nonprofit agency has an outreach program to serve older people. It is operating out of a church in a neighborhood that includes several ethnic minority groups. Staff includes a social worker as case manager/program coordinator and several volunteers who are liaisons between the church and this particular program.

The older female church members, mostly Asian, begin to attend the outreach program because of the church connection. They sew and eat together but also share their experiences and their concerns.

The Client System

As the case manager, you recognize the need for services to expand to the younger generation of these families. However, neither the church nor the central agency has the means for adding personnel or other resources.

You meet with the following group of women:

Mrs. Huang (age 66) is a widow who lives with her son and his three children. She is most interested in having safe recreation facilities for the children. She also states that she will just have to adapt to the modernization of the younger generation. They are "beautiful children but they do not seem to know how to appreciate the opportunities they have as a result of much sacrifice by their parents."

Mrs. Vang (age 63) lives with her daughter, her son-in-law, and two grandchildren. She is in frail health and requires help from her daughter. However, she believes that she contributed to the family when the grandchildren were younger and needed more care. Now, she rarely sees them because they are so busy with school and friends.

Mrs. Nguayen (age 64) was a teacher in her native country. In the U.S., she could only earn a living by cooking and catering Asian food. She is proud of the way in which her children built on that catering opportunity to build a family business. She still cooks but only for a few hours a day. Her time to relax is when she goes to the women's group to sew and talk with the other women.

Mrs. Ho (age 59) is a single parent and still has two unmarried daughters at home. She seems unable to share any concerns.

Ms. Nhan (age 58) is the daughter of another group participant who is now in her late 70s. She works part-time at a daycare center and appears too tired to really interact with the other women. However, she cares for her mother in a loving manner. She is willing to sew and eat with the others, but otherwise seems not to fit in.

Mrs. Nguy (age 68) is a recent immigrant. She is not sure how long it will take her to understand English and this society. Her family saved up to bring her to the United States, and for that she is grateful. However, she does not consider living in the U.S. to be easy. She misses her hometown and the socializing she once did just in the process of going to market each morning. Most of all, she feels guilty for feeling so sad to be here. She wants to be with her children, but she is homesick.

All of the women say they do not feel competent to speak for the entire community. However, they concur on the need to provide a safer environment for children, and on their need to adapt to their more modern grandchildren's values and behaviors. None of the women are interested in working with an advisory committee.

Special Issues

A culturally sensitive intervention is required in order to empower this group to advocate for meeting their needs and the needs of the community.

The case manager/program coordinator has limited skills in the primary language of the women. Cultural and language differences may cause a social worker to be unsure of how to approach sensitive topics.

Key Concepts and Principles

Empowerment

Enabling clients to gain or regain the capacity to interact with the environment in ways that enhance their gratification, well-being, and satisfaction (Hepworth, Rooney, & Larsen, 1997).

Advocacy

The process of working with and on behalf of clients to obtain resources, modify policies, or promote new policies that will result in needed resources and services (Hepworth, Rooney, & Larsen, 1997).

Community organizing

Working with groups of people to bring about change. Change may be brought by working within existing agencies or by working within the broader community.

Suggested Activities

1. Use the client descriptions to role play the women's discussion. Note the language differences and follow the role play with a discussion on the extent to which the women and

staff member effectively communicate. What changes would you suggest if you could repeat this group session?

2. List the strengths of these group participants.

3. Role play how the worker may now approach the staff members and the board of directors to act on the changing needs of this agency's constituency.

4. Discuss the limitation of this sewing/congregate group program. Some individual concerns may be left unattended. How should agency services respond to individual family needs at this point?

5. The group has now become predominantly Vietnamese. Should previous participants from other ethnic groups be recruited? Should separate activities be offered for older women of other groups?

6. Imagine that the board of directors has accepted the idea of having an advisory committee for this outreach program. The worker now takes this mandate to her supervisor for guidance. Since the supervisor had hesitated to take the issues for board consideration at this time, role play a supervisory session in which the worker and her supervisor discuss the status of the situation and how to select potential committee membership for church and women's group consideration.

References and Recommended Reading

Hepworth, D. H., Rooney, R. H., & Larsen J. A. (1997). *Direct social work practice: Theory and skills* (5th ed.). Pacific Grove, CA: Brooks/Cole.

Kirst-Ashman, K. K., & Hull, H. H., Jr. (2001). *Understanding generalist practice* (3rd edition). Chicago, IL: Nelson-Hall.

Kao, R. S., & Lam, M. L., (1997). Asian American elderly. In E. Lee (Ed.), *Working with Asian Americans: A guide for clinicians*. New York: Guilford.

Chapter 16

Involuntary Clients

Involuntary clients, by definition, come to agencies believing they do not have a choice or that the alternatives make their ability not to choose social services only theoretical. When workers acknowledge client feelings about being pressured or coerced, and invite them to participate in planning their time together, clients become less defensive and more empowered to choose within the externally imposed constraints.

Like Mother, Like Daughter

The Agency

You are a medical social worker in the neonatal section of a metropolitan acute care hospital. The hospital has a policy that maternity patients who have a recent history of drug use will have drug screens ordered for their newborns and will be referred to social services. The hospital procedures include the following: (1) the social worker will see the mother for supportive counseling, referral to drug rehabilitation programs, and other appropriate community resources; (2) in the event that the newborn drug screen is positive, Child Protective Services (CPS) will be notified before the baby is discharged home with the mother; (3) for positive screens, instructions from CPS regarding the disposition of the baby's discharge will be followed and documented in the medical record.

The Client System

The day-old infant, Baby Maria, is in the neonatal unit. Her Hispanic mother, Angelica (age 18), appears timid and self-conscious. Paternity of the infant is unknown. When Angelica arrived at the hospital in labor, she disclosed her use of cocaine during pregnancy. Based on that information, the attending physician ordered a drug screen on the infant in compliance with hospital procedures. The results were positive for a trace amount of cocaine. You are contacted by the neonatal charge nurse to carry out the doctor's written order for social services. When you arrive to interview Angelica, she appears frightened and is concerned "my baby will be taken away from me." She says that "Maria is the only person in the world who needs me and I need her."

Special Issues

The mother is a young single parent who wants to care for her child but has no training, limited financial resources, and a history of cocaine use. Angelica did not seek nor even give consent to social work intervention. Therefore, she is a involuntary client with issues that often arise from mandated intervention.

Key Concepts and Principles

Involuntary client
> One who is compelled to partake of the services of a social worker or other professional. Involuntary clients may be mandated (prisoners, persons in institutions, court order) or non-mandated (those pressured by people important to the client) to seek assistance.

Child Protective Services
> Human services, including social, medical, legal, residential, and custodial care, which are provided to children whose caregiver is not providing for their needs.

Medical social worker
> Professional social worker employed in a health care setting primarily to provide for the psychosocial needs of patients and alert other health care providers to the needs of the patient.

Suggested Activities

1. Role play the social worker's first meeting with Angelica, paying particular attention to building rapport and trust.

2. Examine personal and social work ethics involved in this case.

3. Explore policy-making issues that result in mandated clients.

4. Invite a hospital social worker to speak to the class.

References and Recommended Reading

Johnson, H. W. (1998). *The social services: An intro-duction* (5th ed.). Itasca, IL: F. E. Peacock.

Loewenberg, F. M., & Dolgoff, R. (1996). *Ethical decisions for social work practice* (5th ed.). Itasca, IL: F. E. Peacock.

Rothman, J., & Sager, J. S. (1998). *Case manage-ment: Integrating individual and community practice* (2nd ed.). Needham Heights, MA: Allyn and Bacon.

Chapter 17

Worker Safety and Self Care

The formal or informal education of social workers in creating a safe environment for themselves in potentially dangerous situations (e.g., prisons, home visits, detention center, street services). All workers should be made aware of the potential danger to self in the agencies in which they work.

Safety First

The Agency

Apple Blossom Hospice is a 10-year-old agency with a mission to meet the needs of terminally ill patients and their families. In order to receive hospice services, a physician must determine the patient is terminal with a prognosis of less than six months of survival (patients may receive services after the six-month period by a simple recertification process). Hospice services include nursing, pain management, spiritual and religious support, respite for caregivers, and social services. Most services are provided in the home of the patient or patient's family. Two full-time social workers are employed.

The Client System

Suzanne (age 32) is a white female who is in the terminal stage of metastasized breast cancer. The nurse case manager assessed her and at the agency staffing regular social work visits were agreed upon. Your supervisor assigns you the case. When you arrive for the initial home visit to complete a social services assessment, you are greeted at the door by an individual claiming to be the client's brother, a six-foot, muscular male, who in slurred speech tells you his sister is in the living room. As you pass by him, you detect an odor of alcohol. Once in the living room, you greet the client and begin your assessment. The brother enters, and you politely but firmly request privacy with the client. He takes several steps toward you, saying in a loud, menacing voice, "Who do you think you are, coming in here and telling me what to do? Maybe what you need is for me to teach you some respect."

Special Issues

Workers in agencies that provide in-home services are vulnerable to many dangers. Particular attention must be paid to the time of day, neighborhoods, danger signals, escape routes, backup support, pets, and—as in this case—other individuals in the home. Most agencies provide personal safety instruction, but those programs cannot cover all possible circumstances. Safety awareness requires ongoing skill development for all workers.

Key Concepts and Principles

Hospice services
> The provision of health care and homemaker services in nonhospital, home, or home-like settings for individuals with a terminal illness.

Critical incident debriefing
> An approach to understanding and managing the physical and emotional responses of traumatic events. The purpose of the debriefing is to reduce the trauma, initiate an adaptive grief process, and prevent self-defeating behavior.

Suggested Activities

1. Role play the worker's response to the client's brother and the client.

2. Discuss alternatives to the scenario that may have prevented the altercation.

3. Contact a hospice agency and request a copy of the information provided to workers re-

garding safety during home visits, or ask the social worker from the agency to speak to the class.

4. Show a video on safety in home visits (available through most home health agencies) and discuss in class thoughts and feelings evoked by the video.

5. Using the National Association of Social Workers' Code of Ethics as a guide, discuss what the responsibility of the worker is to this client system.

References and Recommended Reading

DuBois, B., & Miley, K. K. (1996). *Social work: An empowering profession.* Needham Heights, MA: Allyn and Bacon.

Thompson, R. A. (1996). *Counseling techniques: Improving relationships with others, ourselves, our families, and our environment.* Bristol, PA: Taylor and Francis.

Chapter 18

Working Within Service Delivery Systems

An awareness of and adherence to the boundaries an agency establishes to meet the needs of clients.

Born in the USA

The Agency

You are an experienced social worker employed by the United Services Association (USA), a small, multiservice agency in River Falls, a city with a population of about 250,000. River Falls has a well-developed social service system, several hospitals and healthcare facilities, and a number of community residences for the mentally ill and persons with developmental disabilities. However, there are no community residences for persons with AIDS, perhaps because the AIDS crisis has been late in affecting this particular community.

The Client System

The chief executive of USA was recently contacted by representatives of two local hospitals to launch a collaborative effort toward establishing a community residence for persons with AIDS. The two hospitals are receiving more HIV positive cases, but neither has discharge planning options for patients who no longer require hospitalization but who are unable to return home. Recently, the state announced funding for programs designed to meet community health needs. The executive director completed the agency's grant application for the project and has asked you to form a multi-agency task group to plan a community residence for persons with AIDS. The executive from USA is expecting a response to the application in about two months. Meanwhile, he thinks the coalition group could begin to plan for establishing the residence and its services. The cooperative effort of the USA's representatives is an important factor in establishing the community residence because the agency would provide a wider resource base to support such an effort and might help overcome the anticipated negative reaction to the residence from members and leaders of this conservative community.

Special Issues

Of concern is the political climate in this conservative community, the obstacles to collaboration by the various agencies and services, the expectations of the parties involved, and the uncertainty of grant funding.

Key Concepts and Principles

Administration in social work
> Methods used by those who have administrative responsibility to determine organizational goals for an agency or other unit, acquire resources and allocate them to carry out a program, coordinate activities, and monitor and assess processes (Barker, 1999).

Collaboration
> The procedure in which two or more professionals work together to serve a client or client system.

Task group
> Any group in which the overriding purpose is to accomplish a goal that is not intrinsically or immediately linked to the needs of the members of the group (Toseland & Rivas, 1998).

Suggested Activities

1. Determine the type of agencies/services/institutions that need to be part of this collaboration in order for it to be successful. Give rationale for choices.

2. Use a problem-solving approach to conduct the initial meeting of representatives from the various agencies. Members of the class represent the various agencies.

3. Discuss the impact of the conservative community in the planning phase of this project, in the implementation phase, and in the evaluation phase.

4. List and discuss specific skills the social worker needs in this situation.

References and Recommended Reading

Barker, R. L. (1999). *The social work dictionary* (4th ed.). Washington, DC: NASW Press.

Corey, M. S., & Corey, G. (1992). *Groups: Process and practice* (4th ed.). Pacific Grove, CA: Brooks/Cole.

Toseland, R. W., & Rivas, R. F. (1998). *An introduction to group work practice.* (3rd ed.). Needham Heights, MA: Allyn and Bacon.

Chapter 19

Crisis Intervention

The therapeutic practice used in helping clients in crisis to promote effective coping that can lead to positive growth and change by acknowledging the problem, recognizing its impact, and learning new or more effective behaviors of coping with similar predictable experiences (Barker, 1999).

ER

The Agency

You are an on-call social worker for the emergency room at St. Stephen's Hospital, a privately owned acute care hospital with an adjacent psychiatric facility. The psychiatric facility does not provide indigent care. Since this hospital is not the primary trauma unit in a midsize metropolitan area, most of the patients seen in St. Stephen's emergency room are there because of suicide attempts, drug and alcohol abuse, indigent care issues, domestic violence, and community resource needs. Your primary focus as the emergency room social worker is crisis intervention. You have approximately one to two hours per case for assessment and referral.

The Client System

The client, Gwendolyn (age 39), is a white female of medium build and weight. She has shoulder-length brown hair which appears unkempt. Although she readily answers all the worker's questions, her affect is flat, her voice is soft, and her eyes are downcast. She is dressed in a hospital gown and is attached to a hospital heart monitor and blood pressure cuff in the "crash" unit of the emergency room. Gwendolyn was brought to the emergency room by ambulance. The client's co-workers found her semi-comatose in her apartment when they checked in on her after she failed to show up for work. According to the client, she had ingested approximately 20 "sleeping pills" and has had her "stomach pumped." The emergency room physician verified a toxic level of benzodiazepine prior to lavage and ordered a social services consultation to assess the patient's mental status and to provide appropriate resource referrals.

Gwendolyn reports that she tried to kill herself because "I can't take it anymore." When asked to elaborate, she indicated that she is all alone, has no family and no friends, and the only meaningful aspect of her life is her job at a local "super variety" store where she manages the pet supplies department. She states that she had been working "off the clock" (i.e., spending more hours at the store after punching out on the time clock) for about six hours every day. She did this because she "enjoyed being at work and did not want to return to the empty apartment where I begin to think about how very lonely I am." Her work supervisor told her she could no longer work after her shift is completed because it is a violation of state labor laws. Gwendolyn reported that "it was the last straw, so I went home and took all the sleeping pills in the bottle." She said she did not think anyone would find her until she was dead, and, "that's what I wanted—to be dead."

During assessment Gwendolyn revealed that she has had feelings of hopelessness for several months and thought she had found a way to avoid those feelings by volunteering extra hours at work. She indicates she has very little appetite, sleeps poorly, and cries easily. She denies any alcohol or drug use. When asked if she has tried to kill herself prior to this attempt, Gwendolyn replied, "I've thought about it a lot, but this is the first time I have actually tried it." She has never been treated for depression and is on no medications except a benzodiazepine, prescribed by her family physician as a sleep aid. When asked if she regretted her actions, she answered, "No, I'm just sorry they found me too soon." However, Gwendolyn also says she "wants to feel better" and is receptive to accepting intervention either as an inpatient or outpatient. She has no health insurance and no financial resources except for a modest savings account.

Special Issues

There is a shortage of community resources for individuals who have no insurance and who do not financially qualify for public assistance. Most facilities require proof of ability to pay if not covered by insurance. A deposit of approximately $1,000 is required prior to admission if the patient is uninsured. Another issue is the short term nature of the intervention in the emergency room where follow-up care is not part of the protocol. In crisis intervention situations such as this one, the beginning, middle and end stages of the helping process are compressed into a short time frame.

Key Concepts and Principles

Crisis process

First, an individual is exposed to stress over a period of time. Second, this stress acts to make the individual exceptionally vulnerable to intimidation and assaults from the outside. Third, a precipitating factor presents itself and acts as a serious threat. Finally, the person experiences surging anxiety. At this point, the person is most receptive to help (Golan, 1996).

Community resources

The agencies, services, and institutions available to eligible clients that can be called upon to help a client's needs.

Suicidal Ideation

Serious contemplation of suicide or thought patterns that lead to killing oneself. Social

workers note specific clues and circumstances to judge the probability that a client is going to attempt suicide (Ivanoff & Riedel, 1995)

Suggested Activities

1. Discuss the responsibility of the social worker in ensuring this client's safety, according to the Social Work *Code of Ethics.*

2. List social policy issues that affect this client's ability to access needed services.

3. Identify ways in which the social worker takes on the roles of counselor, advocate, broker, and educator with this client.

4. Role play how you rapidly assess suicide risk with this client.

5. List the types of community resources available to this client.

References and Recommended Reading

Barker, R. L. (1999). *The social work dictionary* (4th ed.). Washington, DC: NASW Press.

DuBois, B., & Miley, K. K. (1996). *Social work: An empowering profession.* Needham Heights, MA: Allyn and Bacon.

Golan, N. (1996). Crisis theory. In F. J. Turner (Ed.), *Social work treatment: Interlocking theoretical approaches* (4th ed., pp. 168-190). New York: Free Press.

Hoyt, M. F. (1995). *Brief therapy and managed care: Readings for contemporary practice.* San Francisco, CA: Jossey-Bass.

Ivanoff, A., & Riedel, M. (1995). Suicide. In R. L. Edwards (Editor-in-Chief), *Encyclopedia of social work* (19th ed., pp. 2358-2372). Washington, DC: NASW Press.

Lowenburg, F. M., & Dolgoff, R. (1996). *Ethical decisions for social work practice* (5th ed.). Itasca, IL: F. E. Peacock.

Borderlines

The Agency

A mid-sized city has just established a victims assistance program within its Police Department. This new counseling and crisis intervention resource is designed for the provision of crisis counseling to victims of crime. The three social workers and consulting psychiatrist usually carry cases for no more than six weeks and frequently refer clients to other community services if treatment is to last longer or requires some other type of service. An additional pool of clients comes from officer referrals of persons who "abuse" police services in apparent attention-getting patterns (e.g., persons who live alone and repeatedly call to report noise disturbances or harassment by their neighbors or their neighbors' pets). Also, as staff workload permits, referrals are accepted from the justice of the peace for city jail inmates requiring immediate assessment of suicidal ideation, release with a stipulation of mandatory counseling, or both.

The Client System

Police were called to the Sosa home by an unidentified young male who claimed there had been a shooting in his home. Upon arrival, the officer found Mr. Sosa (age 45) fatally shot, Mrs. Sosa (age 42) badly bruised and shaken, and three children—Bob (age 17), John (age 12), and Nathan (age 10). The other children, twins Katy and Cathy (age 19), live in an apartment they have shared since high school graduation a year ago. According to the officer in charge, the shooting occurred while Mr. Sosa was verbally and physically abusing his wife, as he frequently did while under the influence of alcohol. Bob fre-

quently intervened by sheltering his mother and assisting her exit from the room. Since Mr. Sosa never struck his children, he usually retreated to his bedroom until he was sober again. This time, however, Bob was not able to assist his mother and according to Mrs. Sosa, "Suddenly, Bob left the room, returned with his father's gun, and shot and killed his father."

Although Bob was the person who called emergency services, he refused to talk to the police, giving only curt responses to questions regarding the incident. The officer noted that Mrs. Sosa would often come to her son's aid in answering questions about the family violence. He also noticed that the daughters and the mother did not appear to hold any animosity towards Bob. He checked and verified that Bob had a "clean record" and had never been violent in the past. The police officer refers the case to you, one of the victims assistance counselors.

When you arrive, the family appears calm. The daughters and Mrs. Sosa are contacting family and friends, Bob is standing by but uncommunicative, and the younger boys are out of sight but somewhere in the house. Mrs. Sosa shares her concern about Bob "being so quiet and keeping things to himself." She plans to go to the doctor to have a swollen arm x-rayed, and has called a family attorney to help with business matters and any legal problems that might emerge for Bob.

Special Issues

Working with law enforcement presents the practitioner with the challenge of establishing trust with both the client system and with the police officers when an alleged crime has occurred. Adherence to agency policies and procedures becomes of paramount importance in order to maintain a positive working relationship with both the community and law enforcement. In addition, the practitioner is often placed in a crisis situation requiring skilled intervention.

Key Concepts and Principles

Victims assistance
> Crisis intervention, short term services offered to crime survivors and people related to crime victims.

Suggested Activities

1. Discuss the cycle of violence that characterizes wife battering.
2. Role play your initial contact with the officer in charge, keeping in mind the collaborative atmosphere you are to maintain with all officers.
3. Role play three consecutive sessions with the Sosas: (a) the initial session in the home, just after the shooting; (b) the following day, while the family makes funeral arrangements; and (c) two days later, following the funeral.
4. Assume three separate ethnic identities for this family and use a culturagram for assessment and empowerment.
5. Discuss special issues relevant to the introduction of an interpreter, and role play one of the consecutive sessions with an interpreter.

References and Recommended Reading

Congress, E. P. (1994). The use of culturagrams to assess and empower culturally diverse families. *Families in Society, 75*, 531-540.

Kirst-Ashman, K. K., & Hull, H. H., Jr. (1999). *Understanding generalist practice* (2nd ed.). Chicago, IL: Nelson-Hall.